THE GREAT
ANTIQUES TREASURE HUNT

Test Your Knowledge of Antiques and Collectibles
and Learn While You Search

COMPILED BY

PAUL ATTERBURY

HARRY N. ABRAMS, INC., PUBLISHERS

CONTENTS

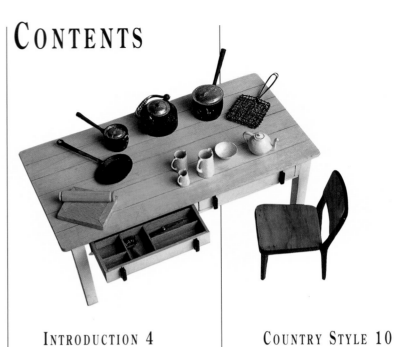

ISBN 0–8109–3378–0

Copyright © 1993 Marshall Editions
Developments Ltd.

Published in 1993 by Harry N. Abrams,
Incorporated, New York
A Times Mirror Company

The Great Antiques Treasure Hunt is a
Marshall Edition

Printed and bound in Italy

Valuation is an imprecise art and prices can
vary for many reasons, including condition
of a piece, fashion, and national and regional
tastes. Prices given in this book are
approximate and based on likely *auction*
values. *Insurance* values reflect the retail
replacement price and as such are liable to
be higher.

The publishers would like to thank
John C. Benjamin of Phillips auctioneers
for his invaluable help with the jewelry
section on pages 16–19

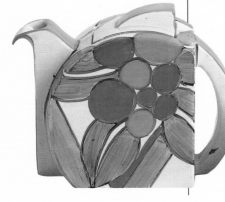

INTRODUCING
THE GREAT ANTIQUES TREASURE HUNT

Antique collecting is all about hunting – the tracking down of that rare and
elusive object, the searching for the vital background information
that will confirm the attribution, and the moment of triumph when the
object is finally captured. And, as every collector knows,
so much is a matter of luck.

For a true collector, the excitement of stepping into a crowded antique shop
and scanning the cluttered shelves is one that never dies. Every shop
or market stall is a new thrill, full of possibilities and promise, and a challenge
to the eye and the memory. The pages of this book are a series of
splendid and richly stocked antique shops, packed with hidden treasures.

Every object tells a story, but some have more to say than others, and
the challenge is to pick these out. Each page is a treasure trove
of secrets waiting to be discovered – the only clues are a set of questions
and brief descriptions. The rest is up to you, to your eye, your memory and
your imagination. All the excitement of the chase is here, in areas both
familiar and unfamiliar, and there are plenty of opportunities to test
your knowledge – and your luck.

Here are a thousand ways of building in your imagination some of the
best collections in the world, with all the pleasures of the hunt but with none
of the worries about display, storage, insurance, condition and, above all else,
the cost. As these pages fill your mind with all those things you might one
day acquire, enjoy the knowledge gained along the route. Remember, when
it comes to the antiques trail, knowledge is power. Good hunting.

Paul Atterbury

THE TREASURE HUNT BEGINS HERE

Set before you on these pages is a mass of objects from each of
twelve major collecting areas – spanning furniture to glass, and
militaria to china. Accompanying each collage is a series of
questions to test your wits.

To help you answer the questions a "decoder" gives a brief definition
of each piece, explaining what it is, when it was made and its
probable worth. It also highlights any special features
that may help you in your quest.

When your eye has finished roaming each delightful
collection, and you think you have the solution, turn
to the back of the book, where you will find
the answers given in full.

BLUE-AND-WHITE BAZAAR

1 Find something for the desk, for the bathroom, for bulbs and for flavoring.

2 Where is an edible Japanese delicacy?

3 Where was the famous willow pattern invented? Search out examples, and find the odd one out.

4 Which is the most valuable piece and how much would it cost?

5 Locate and find uses for a garniture and some lambrequins.

6 Find something inspired by the art of a lost Italian city and a Meissen imposter.

7 Find receptacles to capture the spirit of Scotland and the fire of France.

8 Which piece is associated with some well-known baggage?

9 Locate two North African beasts of burden.

10 Find a lady taking tea and a gentleman teeing off.

BLUE-AND-WHITE BAZAAR

1 Staffordshire meat dish with pattern "Chinese Juvenile Sports" and floral border **(1a)**. 1825. 19in. **(B)**

2 Pickle dish from Limehouse in London; the first factory producing English blue and white porcelain. 1748. 4¼in. **(E)**

3 Three Chinese dinner plates **(3a,b)** from the vast quantity made for export to Europe during the 18th century. Typical designs **(3c–e)**. 1750–75. 7–9in. Each **(A)**

4 Japanese Hirado porcelain rat on a radish. 1860–80. 7in. **(C)**

5 "Kraak" dish with bird centerpiece **(5a)** and painted border **(5b,c)**. Kraak is the earliest exported Chinese porcelain and takes its name from the carrack it sailed in. *c.*1620. 14in. **(C)**

6 Spill vase or brush pot made in China. 1880. 11in. **(B)**

7 Japanese Arita dish copied from a Chinese "Kraak" original; the design is obscured by the glaze **(7a–c)**. 1660–80. 14in. **(E)**

8 Chinese jar painted with rambling prunus flowers **(8b,c)** on a blue "cracked ice" ground. It has a decorated knop **(8a)** and neck **(8d)**. Late 1900s. 13in high. **(C)**

9 Hanau faience ginger jar and cover. Made in Holland to resemble Chinese porcelain. *c.*1710. 12in. **(G)**

10 Chinese plate painted with typical motifs and patterned border detail **(10a–e)**. 1770. 8½in. **(A)**

11 Ming tea bowl, bearing the mark of Emperor Yung-lo. *c.*1403–24. 3¾in. **(G)**

12 Liverpool painted tile depicting English rural landscape. Other design **(12a)**. 1800s. 6in. **(B)**

13 Dynasty marks from Chinese porcelain: Ch'ing emperor Yung-cheng, 1723–35 **(13)**; Ming emperor Ch'eng-hua, 1465–87 **(13a,e)**; Ming emperor Hsüan-te, 1426–35 **(13b,d)**; Ch'ing emperor K'ang-hsi, 1662–1722 **(13c)**.

14 Transfer-printed Staffordshire pearlware punch bowl. 1820. 11in. **(B)**

15 Chinese jar with dramatic dragon and phoenix designs in vivid blue **(15a,b)**. 1425–50. 5in. **(G)**

16 Transfer-printed Staffordshire bowl with picturesque scene from English country life. Interior **(16a)** 1840. 9in. **(A)**

17 Classic willow pattern plate by Dillwyn and Co. of Swansea, Wales. Many misleading legends have been attributed to the motifs **(17a–f)** which are purely artistic. 1820–30. 10in. **(A)**

18 Delftware bowl decorated with a view of the Tower of London. Called after the Dutch town of Delft where it was copied from Chinese exports. Detail **(18a)**. 1600. 11in. **(G)**

19 Two Chinese meat dishes with gilded edges **(19b,c)** from a dinner service. Detail **(19a)**. 1760–80. 14in and 13in. **(C)**

20 Meissen cream pot in experimental underglaze blue; this technique was not a success for the German company and so pieces are rare. Knop on cover **(20a)**. 1730. 5in. **(E)**

21 Japanese tea or punch pot from Arita. 1720. 7in. **(F)**

22 Date marks from English Worcester china pieces: 1903 **(22)**; 1937 **(22a)**; 1873 **(22b)**; 1890 **(22c)**.

23 W&R Ridgway meat dish with a printed lotus pattern **(23a)** and unusual "lobed" edge **(23b)**. 1830. 15in. **(B)**

24 Florian ware vases by English designer William Moorcroft, in his "Pompeii" shape **(24a,b)**. 1903. 4in. **(D)**

25 Pearlware "bell" custard cup by English potters Spode, used for desserts. 1810. 2in. **(A)**

26 French St. Cloud cup and saucer with undulating reeding **(26a)**. 1730. Saucer 5in. **(B)**

27 Staffordshire meat dish with unusual pattern based on a textile design **(27a–h)**. 1820. 20½in. **(C)**

28 Chamber pot **(28b,d)** and covered dishes **(28a,c)** from an earthenware bedroom set by Thomas Lawrence of Longton, England. 1925. **(A)**

55b

PRICE CODE: **A** less than $200 **B** $200–400 **C** $400–750 **D** $750–1,500 **E** $1,500–3,000 **F** $3,000–5,000 **G** over $5,000

29 Date marks from Minton china and earthenware: 1891–1912 **(29)**; 1845–72 **(29a)**; 1800–15 **(29b)**; 1860–69 **(29c)**; 1850s **(29d)**; pattern number from 1812 **(29e)**.

30 Chinese salt dish or "salt." 1770. 3in. **(A)**

31 Beaker vase made in the "Transitional" period, at the end of the Ming dynasty, with typical shape, figures and purplish tone of blue **(31a)**. 1620–44. 16½in. **(G)**

32 Commemorative plate showing the popular British Prime Minister William Gladstone (1809–98) **(32a)**. 1880s. 10in. **(A)**

33 Meat dish with crest and initials. 1780s. 18in. **(C)**

34 Chinese teapot with floral pattern in underglaze blue. Details of lid **(34a)** and spout **(34b)**. Mid-17th C. 4in. **(B)**

35 Chinese "Kraak" porcelain dish with segmented border **(35a)** and traditional knot motifs **(35c–e)** surrounding a central scene of flowers and birds **(35b)**. 1600. 19in. **(F)**

36 Novelty gift plate with calendar in lavender underglaze for Liverpool company J.W. Harrison **(36a,b)**. 1878. 8in. **(A)**

37 Date marks from French Sèvres porcelain: 1845–48 **(37)**; painter's mark of Dodin 1754–1802 **(37a)**; 1756 **(37b)**; 1778 **(37c)**; painter's mark of Le Guay 1778–1840 **(37d)**.

38 Giant willow pattern cup, with a mercury-gilt rim **(38a)** and ornate ring-handle **(38b)**. 1880. 4½in high. **(A)**

39 Chinese pen tray made in the reign of the Ming Emperor Wan-li. Date mark **(39a–d)**. 1573–1619. 7½in. **(G)**

40 Set of Chinese soup and sauce tureens made for export. Decoration **(40a)**. Mid-18th C. Largest one 16 x 12in. **(C)**

41 Sauce tureen, one of a pair, made in China as part of a complete dinner service. Late 19th C. 9in. **(E)**

42 Set of four willow patterned spirit decanters made in England. Other decanters **(42a–c)**. Early 19th C. 8in. Set **(C)**

43 Shallow "Kraak" bowl with traditional aster and fan symbols **(43a)** on the border panels. 1640. 11in. **(E)**

44 English Delftware copy of Ming dish. 1635. 12in. **(F)**

45 Staffordshire meat dish decorated with Chinese mythical beasts **(45a–d)**. 1825. 19in. **(C)**

46 Pearlware ribbon plate with pierced border for a ribbon. Detail of centerpiece design **(46a)**. 1795. 7½in. **(B)**

47 Chinese export dish with temple landscape featuring a pagoda, bridge and boats **(47a)**. 1770. 16 x 12½in. **(C)**

48 Bow plate from London with knapped border **(48a–c)** and golfer and caddy design **(48d–g)** based on a Chinese original of a sage and his servant. *c.*1755–60. 8in. **(E)**

49 Chinese vase from a matching group of five; different shapes **(49a,d)** enable them to sit closely together **(49b)**. Decorative panels **(49c)**. 1780. 12in. **(C)**

50 Earthenware plate commissioned to commemorate the coronation of British monarch George V. 1911. 9in. **(A)**

51 Breakfast service by Wood and Baggaley in "Flo" blue with gilding. Tea cup **(51a)**. Jug **(51b)**. Early 19th C. **(A)**

57a

52 Japanese Fukagawa vase with mountain landscape in underglaze blue. 1900s. 11in. **(D)**

53 Bridge, bird **(53a)** and boat **(53b)** motifs from a willow pattern plate. 18th C.

54 Chinese teapot based on a silver design, with gilding on body and spout **(54a)** added later in England. *c.*1790. 5in. **(C)**

55 Underglaze blue teapot with neoclassical shape and picture of the owner taking tea in her garden. Spout **(55a)**. Obverse side **(55b)**. 1781. 5½in. **(D)**

56 Top of ewer by English makers Doulton with blue and white narcissi and gilt leaves. Ewer **(56a)**. 1895. 12in. **(B/C)**

57 Wedgwood candlestick dipped in jasper, a stoneware fired at a high temperature. Pair **(57a)**. 1840. 9in. Pair **(B/C)**

58 Quintal vase, so called because of the five joined vases surrounding its central stem **(58a)**. 1870. 9in. **(C)**

59 Pearlware plate with oriental scene of figures, rafts and pagodas **(59a,b)**. 1800. 9½in. **(A)**

60 Rare shield-shaped flask from 17th-century China depicting a warrior in underglaze blue **(60a)**. 1650. 7in. **(C)**

61 Butter dish in the shape of a shell. 1750. 5in. Pair **(D)**

62 Powder blue panel vases by William Moorcroft. The slip-trailed decoration is inspired by oriental ceramics **(62a)**. 1915. 12in. Pair **(E)**

63 Miniature cup and saucer by Minton. Detail **(63a)**. 1860. 2in. **(A)**

64 Ewer and basin by English makers Gater, Hall & Co. with gilt borders. 1914. 14in. **(A)**

65 Spode earthenware plate with exotic, North African scene. 1815. 9in. **(A)**

66 Wedgwood pearlware jug with printed flowers and gilded details. 1805. 7½in. **(C)**

67 Chinese dish with mountain scene and border of painted prunus. 1890. 16in. **(B)**

68 Oriental dish with wand patterns imported into Europe. 18th C. 15in. **(B)**

69 Florian ware vase with slip-trailed design in shades of blue **(69a,c,d)** and triangular handles **(69b)**. 1904. 12in. **(E)**

70 Tureen from a Sèvres dessert service decorated by the celebrated flower painter Michaud. 1790. 4in high. **(C)**

71 Maker's mark of leaf within two circles from an 18th-century Chinese dish.

72 Mark of German makers Sitzendorf intended to resemble Meissen. A more individual mark **(72a)**.

73 Bee design from fine Chelsea porcelain plate. Further examples **(73a,b)**. 1755–60.

74 Flower and bird **(74a)** details from Derby chestnut basket. *c.*1760.

56a

COUNTRY STYLE

1 Which chests or coffers are used to store blankets, a chamber pot and baker's dough?

2 Name three popular woods used for country-made furniture, and find an example of each.

3 What would you do with a canterbury?

4 Samplers are now in great demand, but of what were they a sample, and which of the three shown remains true to that aim?

5 "Religion in Wood." Which three pieces of furniture reflect the pious ideals of one American community?

6 The wood for one of the chairs shown here came from the sea. Which one is it and what is kept in the drawer?

7 Which Windsor chair was made farthest from England's royal castle?

1 The East exerted a strong artistic influence worldwide. Find English, French and American examples.

2 Find textiles made in three oriental countries.

3 Identify three examples of inlay work using different materials. What are the names of the techniques?

4 Find an inro, a netsuke and an okimono. What was each used for in everyday life?

5 Which three *objets d'art* were made or decorated in the East to satisfy western tastes?

6 Eastern craftsmen incorporated many animal products. Find three examples, crafted from four different natural materials.

7 Birds exert a special fascination for eastern craftsmen. Find a crane, a goose and an eagle.

8 Which piece is the most valuable?

9 Find a games player.

MYSTERIES OF THE EAST

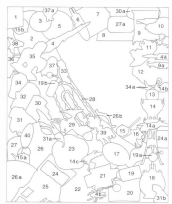

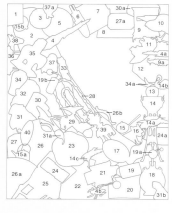

1a

1 Door from a miniature Japanese cabinet (1a) made from sheets of ivory and lacquered in gold and black. c.1880. 7in. (F)

2 Chinese fisherman carved in ivory with detailing in black; represents an "immortal" or minor Buddhist deity. 19th C. 19in. (C)

3 Armorial plate made in China with an unusual waved border. 1740. 8¼in. (E)

4 Chinese lettuce, radish (4a) and grasshopper (4b) carved in ivory and colored with vegetable dyes. 1920. 8in. (D)

5 Armorial charger, or serving plate, made in China. c.1760. 17in wide. (G)

6 Japanese wooden toggle in the shape of a bearded sage holding a basket. 1750. 4in high. (B)

7 Fall-front desk made in the East from rosewood; the rippling effect is a Dutch influence. c.1760. 5ft high. (G)

8 Indian bridge cloth with a wide chain-stitched border sewn onto a velvet background. 1850–60. 3ft 3in. (C)

9 Japanese display cabinet or "shodana" containing asymetrically arranged cupboards and drawers, and decorated with fine lacquerwork (9a). c.1900. 3ft 8in wide. (G)

10 Bronze pheasant from Japan with dark patination and details picked out in copper and gold. 1890. 12in. (E)

11 Small ivory carving of five peasants on a boat journey. Deliberately aged by staining it with sepia. 1900. 2in. (C)

12 Japanese wall hanging in fine floss silks on a satin ground with birds, flowers and maples. c.1910. 4 x 5ft. (C)

13 Peasant's head with comical expression from an early Japanese ivory sculpture. The complete figure depicts a struggle with an oversized radish – a popular subject in Japanese humor. 1800. 1½in high. (C)

14 Jardinière, or flower stand, in the Japanese style with gilt bronze celestial clouds and wave and crane motifs (14a–c), supported by a mock bamboo pedestal. 1874. 5ft 3in. (G)

15 Fine Japanese-style tea set made of iron and decorated with flowers and sea creatures in gold and silver alloys. Kettle (15a). Sugar bowl (15b). 1883. (E)

16 Porcelain tiger from China. 1850s. 6in. (C)

17 Colorful vase and bowl set decorated with dragons, the Chinese symbol for regeneration. 1930s. Bowl 11in wide. Vase 13in tall. (B)

18 Japanese-style moonflask decorated in a traditional oriental pattern of wild flowers in blue and green enamel. 1870s. 11in. (D)

19 Japanese kimono accessories, consisting of two multi-layered boxes for small daily items lacquered in gold and held together by a toggle (19a). (19) 1850. 4in. (C); (19b) 1820. 4in. (D)

20 Embroidered panel depicting two Turkish gentlemen; worked in silk and metal threads. 1780–1820. 21in. (C)

21 Japanese miniature chest of drawers or "kodansu" made by Komai, who specialized at inlaying gold into iron. 1900. 3in high. (F)

22 Japanese cabinet decorated with inlaid woods. The raised lid shows Mount Fuji in lacquerwork. Late 19th C. 17in. (B)

23 Chinese cinnabar lacquer box. Early 19th C. 10in. (D)

24 Watchcase lacquered in Japan and depicting a galloping samurai warrior (24a). 1920s. 3in. (D)

25 Chinese-made worktable with lacquer finish in two tones of gold with a workbag beneath. 1830–50. 2ft 5in. (F)

26 Japanese moonflask showing a carp turning into a dragon as it leaps a waterfall (26a), symbolic of a student passing exams. Handle (26b). 1860s. 13in. (D)

27 Lady's ivory workbox, made in China, with fitments for winding silks and sewing (27a). 1850s. 12in. (E)

28 Japanese damascene necklace, inlaid with gold and decorated with good luck symbols. 1910. 16in. (A)

29 Three ivory kingfishers on a lotus pad made from a stag's antler by the Japanese carver Kofu. 1900. 11in. (G)

30 Three Chinese brush pots. Detail (30a). 1900. 4–6in. (A)

31 Japanese figurine of Daikoku, god of farming, with silver, mother-of-pearl and lacquer. Details (31a,b). 1870. 1in. (E)

32 "The Sack of Happiness" carving in wood from Japan, signed Kanshu. Opens to reveal Hotei, god of happiness, playing Go with a small boy. 1765. 1in. (D)

33 Walrus ivory fisherman with Raiden, god of thunder. Made by the Tamayuki studio in Japan. 1900. 12in. (C)

34 Japanese bronze vase with a flying bird emblem (34a) inlaid in gold and silver alloy. 1900. 9in. (B)

35 Pottery money box in the shape of an elephant and castle. c.1790. 8in. high (G)

36 Indian worktable in elaborately carved and pierced rosewood. 1830–60. 20in. (E)

37 Miniature figure in ivory of a Japanese drum seller. Detail (37a). 1890. 2in. (B/C)

38 Dragon-shaped handle from a Japanese ornamental ewer in enamel and gilt. Complete ewer (38a). 1832. 8in. (G)

39 Oriental elephant in ebony with inlaid silver-mounted casket. c.1900. 14in. (G)

40 Enamel cup cover. 1920s. 7in. With cup (C)

38a

JEWELRY BOX

1 Find a dragonfly which is not a fairy; a lion; and a dove looking at a cross.

2 Which gemstone is reminiscent of the seas and oceans? Find three examples.

3 Locate a pair of cuff links made by a famous Russian goldsmith.

4 Find two pieces depicting the god Apollo drawing the chariot of the sun. What are they made of?

5 Which reptile carries a pearl on his back, and to which pendant does he give his backing?

6 Which brooch has been plucked from a chicken?

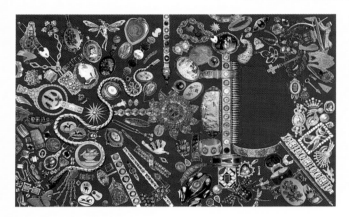

109

1 Gold brooch set with a diamond and two rubies in a star design **(1a)**, flanked by beadwork. 1885. **(A)**

2 Sapphire and diamond flower brooch. 1880. **(F)**

3 Art Deco diamond plaque pendant set with ruby flowers and emerald leaves. Diamond link **(3a)**. 1920. **(G)**

4 English gold seal hanging from an elongated oval link and embossed hooplike chain. 1865. **(D)**

5 Diamond 16-ray star brooch set with a sapphire. 1885. **(F)**

6 Agate cameo portrait brooch in an Etruscan-style gold mount **(6a)**. Details of cameo **(6b,c)**. 1880. **(D)**

7 Victorian music brooch made by Hunt and Roskell, Queen Victoria's jewelers. Complete with case **(7a)**. 1870. **(C/D)**

8 Maltese gold locket with a rose-cut diamond flower spray centerpiece **(8a)**. Attachment **(8b)**. 1860s. **(D)**

9 French or Swiss gold and enamel pendant. 1890. **(C)**

10 Art Nouveau maiden brooch in gold, with gem encrusted and *plique à jour* enamel wings. 1900. **(G)**

11 Tortoiseshell *piqué* pendant set with gold and mother-of-pearl designs. Hanging support **(11a)**. 1880. **(A)**

12 Gold beadwork brooch with a single diamond. 1880. **(C)**

13 Carved ivory hand clenching a hardstone and gold baton with seal. Made in England. 1845. **(F)**

14 Frosted 15ct gold bracelet with banded agates set in a neoclassical shell design border. Banded agate **(14a,c)**; in setting **(14b)**. 1900. **(D)**

15 Fabergé enamel, sapphire and gold torpedo cuff link with *guilloché* enameling. Other cuff link **(15a)**. 1895. **(G)**

16 Diamond and ruby brooch. 1915. **(E)**

17 Gold pendant, inset with portrait miniature. 1905. **(A)**

18 Bracelet with carved lava plaques **(18a)** mounted in gold. 1850. **(C/D)**

19 Mourning brooch with a lock of hair **(19a)** held by a seed pearl clasp. 1865. **(B)**

20 Passion-flower brooch made of paste to simulate emeralds, amethysts, topaz and diamonds. 1760. **(E)**

21 Gem and clasp from a garnet **(21a)** and gold bracelet by John Brogden **(21c)**. Linking gold baton **(21b)**. 1865. **(F)**

22 Gold tablet-section serpent necklace, set with various semi-precious stones. 1875. **(F)**

23 Onyx cameo of Apollo Belvedere. 1870. **(D)**

24 Hollow-link gold bracelet with a tiny padlock **(24a)** and set with semi-precious stones. 1900s. **(B/C)**

25 Shell cameo engraved with biblical scene. 1880–90. **(B)**

26 Italian cameo set in a gold mount. 1860–80. **(C)**

27 Hinged gold bangle with micro-mosaic classical scene and the motto ROMA. 1880. **(G)**

28 Italian brooch with classical-style cameo scene held in a gold mount inset with turquoise **(28a–c)**. 1830. **(E)**

29 Victorian chased-gold panel bracelet set with amethysts, aquamarines and citrines. 1875. **(E)**

30 Victorian gold teardrop fringe necklace. 1880. **(F)**

31 Transfer-printed porcelain plaque set in a gilt brooch mount. 1880–90. **(A/B)**

32 Victorian diamond 12-ray star brooch. 1875. **(F)**

33 Bakelite bangle in translucent red. 1940–45. **(A)**

34 Diamond, sapphire and ruby peacock brooch. 1950. **(G)**

35 Ruby and diamond *pavé* cluster clip. 1930. **(G)**

36 Garnet cabochon and gold hinged bangle. 1865. **(E)**

37 Gold wishbone brooch, with ruby **(37a)**, diamond and sapphire **(37b)**. Made in South Africa. 1880. **(C)**

38 Art Nouveau style 9ct gold pendant, set with half pearls and garnets **(38a,b)**. 1900–10. **(B)**

39 Red enamel and gold Imperial Order. 1880. **(C)**

40 Opal and diamond ring. Detail **(40a)**. 1920. **(C)**

41 Burmese ruby and diamond ring. Ruby **(41a)**. 1985. **(G)**

42 Van Cleef & Arpels caliber ruby brooch in the shape of a leaf. 1930. **(G)**

51a

77b

PRICE CODE: **A** less than $200 **B** $200–400 **C** $400–750 **D** $750–1,500 **E** $1,500–3,000 **F** $3,000–5,000 **G** over $5,000

7a

43 Glass bead necklace. 1940. *(A)*

44 Unmounted Burmese ruby and obverse **(44a)**. 1985. *(G)*

45 Wooden sailor brooch with leather sail **(45a)**. Made in the U.S. 1940. *(A)*

46 Coral grotesque brooch. 1865. *(D)*

47 Celluloid fox-head buckle. 1940. *(A)*

48 Gold crossover ring with diamonds and rubies. 1912. *(C)*

49 Gold pendant with amphora drop and center set with seed pearls. 1880. *(D)*

50 Emerald and diamond arrow *sûreté* pin. 1910. *(E)*

51 Spider from a bar brooch **(51a)** featuring a spider and fly inset with a pearl and pink tourmaline. 1900. *(A/B)*

52 Diamond and onyx coronet brooch. 1910. *(E)*

53 Gold brooch with vari-color agate cameo. 1790. *(E)*

54 Platinum and diamond brooch and detail **(54a)**. 1950. *(G)*

55 Pearl and diamond ear-clip. Other clip **(55a)**. 1965. *(F)*

56 Diamond ring between diamond shoulders. 1985. *(G)*

57 Dragon buckle in carved and pierced white bakelite and diamanté. Dragon's wing **(57a)**. 1940. *(A)*

58 Brilliant- and baguette-cut diamond coil and cascade brooch. Central motif **(58a)**. 1955. *(E)*

59 Geometric platinum and diamond bracelet. 1950. *(G)*

60 Step-cut line bracelet in Burmese rubies. 1935. *(G)*

61 Etruscan-style bangle with micro-mosaic panels **(61b,c)** and *salve* (salvation) in gold on the reverse **(61a)**. 1870. *(E)*

62 Half-hoop opal and diamond ring in retailer's box. Hand-carved gold mount **(62a)**. 1911. *(B)*

63 Diamond, ruby and emerald bracelet. 1925. *(G)*

64 Diamond Saint Esprit brooch with emerald drop. 1865. *(E)*

65 Articulated diamond dragonfly brooch with flat-cut peridot wings. 1895. *(G)*

66 Diamond and emerald bee brooch with ruby eyes in gold and silver mount. Thorax **(66a)**. Wing **(66b)**. 1860. *(G)*

67 Heart-shaped locket with raised diamond and pearl center **(67a)** and green enamel surround. 1900. *(D)*

68 Hinged gold bangle with wirework design. 1885. *(D)*

69 Art Deco style diamond, emerald and onyx ring. 1985. *(F)*

70 Maltese 18ct gold bangle with mosaics of country people in local costume **(70a,b)** set in malachite. 1870. *(E)*

71 Emerald drop earring with diamond surround. Other earring **(71a)**. 1950. Pair *(E)*

72 Peridot and gold pendant. 1875. *(G)*

73 Green enamel, gold and ruby frog brooch. 1960. *(D)*

74 Crescent-shaped gold brooch set with diamonds and opals. 1900. *(C)*

75 Brooch with *pavé* and baguette diamonds and drop-shaped sapphires. 1950. *(G)*

76 "Albert" watch chain with tassles. 1860. *(E)*

77 Centerpiece of a bar brooch with

die-stamped surround **(77a,b)**. 1904. *(A)*

78 Gold brooch set with rose-cut diamonds **(78a,b)**. Border **(78c)**. 1880. *(B)*

79 Edwardian bar brooch with half-pearls and overlaid with a diamond and ruby scroll. 1905. *(B)*

80 Diamond strap bracelet set with multicolored gems. 1935. *(G)*

81 Amethyst and gold hinged panel bracelet. 1865. *(G)*

82 Art Deco fire opal and diamond clip. 1910. *(F)*

83 Boat-shaped sapphire and diamond cluster ring in a platinum mount. Sapphires **(83a–c)**. 1915. *(D)*

84 Gold and turquoise padlock locket clasp. 1845. *(D)*

85 Gold cuff links with enameled racehorses **(85a)**. 1930. *(D)*

86 Gold turtle brooch with baroque pearl body. 1890. *(C)*

87 Pliny's Doves micro-mosaic brooch. Detail **(87a)**. 1850. *(F)*

88 Art Deco sapphire and diamond cuff link. Other cuff link **(88a)**. Details of face design **(88b–d)**. 1935. *(G)*

89 Blue glass earrings imitating lapis lazuli. 1920s. *(A)*

90 Sapphire cabochon and diamond dress ring. 1920. *(E)*

91 Sapphire dress ring with diamond shoulders. 1965. *(G)*

92 Art Nouveau enameled silver pendant. 1909. *(B)*

93 Star sapphire and diamond pendant. 1930. *(G)*

94 Gold serpent necklace with blue enamel, diamond and ruby head and articulated body. 1845. *(F)*

95 Aquamarine pendant earrings **(95a)**. 1950. *(G)*

96 Enameled silver butterfly brooch. Wing **(96a)**. 1920s. *(A)*

97 Gold *pavé* turquoise coiled serpent bangle. 1845. *(F)*

98 Aquamarine and diamond plaque brooch. 1950. *(G)*

99 Art Nouveau enameled pendant with integral chain by Charles Horner. Detail **(99a)**. 1909. *(B)*

100 Aquamarine **(100a)** and diamond pendant. 1950. *(G)*

101 Gold *pavé* turquoise serpent bracelet. 1845. *(F)*

102 Aquamarine **(102a)** and diamond dress ring. 1950s. *(G)*

103 Cluster ring with sapphire and diamonds. 1965. *(G)*

104 Sapphire and diamond dress ring. 1965. *(G)*

105 Gold bracelet folding into miniature book, the spine set with turquoise **(105a,b)**. 1850. *(F)*

106 Ring mounted with a sapphire and diamonds. 1985. *(G)*

107 Mourning ring enameled in turquoise blue. 1808. *(B)*

108 Georgian diamond ring set in silver and gold. *c.*1790. *(D)*

109 Diamond and caliber ruby wristwatch. 1925. *(F)*

110 Florentine plaque brooch made from *pietra dura* in 15ct gold mount **(110c)**. Details **(110a,b)**. 1850. *(C)*

111 French diamond collar with detachable centerpiece **(111a)**. 1930. *(G)*

112 Embossed gold pendant set with mother-of-pearl cameo. 1780. *(D)*

113 Brooch with basket of flowers of multicolored gemstones. 1950. *(G)*

21c

110c

1 Many instruments shown here enlarge images; but which one is capable of both enlarging and reducing?

2 Which devices would help you to find your way at sea, in outer space and underground?

3 Locate two early devices used to receive important messages.

4 Which two instruments, one navigational and one climatic, have polar associations?

5 Which instruments measure direction, distance, weight and temperature?

6 Not all these instruments have a practical purpose. Which three are devised purely for pleasure and entertainment?

7 What do a banjo, stick, aneroid and wheel have in common: what do they predict?

8 Find an instrument with a peaceful purpose in time of war.

WONDERS OF SCIENCE

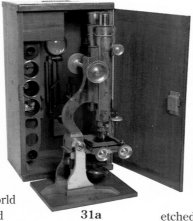

2a

1 Block instrument used by British signalmen of the Great Central Railway to determine if a line was clear. When the handle was pulled (**1a,b**) a telegraphic signal indicated one of three possibilities on a colored dial (**1c**). 1900. 2ft 6in. **(A/B)**

2 Jupiter and moons section from a rare orrery, or model of the solar system, by William and Samuel Jones of London. Complete orrery (**2a**). 1810. 5in high. **(G)**

3 Exotic singing bird automata mounted in a gilded cage with Art Nouveau designs (**3a**). Made in France. *c.*1900. 20in high. **(E)**

4 Pocket set of compass (**4a**), thermometer (**4b**) and aneroid barometer (**4c**) in a crocodile-skin case. This English-made device was used by walkers. 1885–90. Case 3 x 4in. **(C)**

5 Thermometer from a priceless collection of scientific instruments used to record extreme weather conditions. Other items include a sundial (**5a**), compass (**5b**), altitude scale (**5c**) and aneroid barometer (**5d**). 1910. **(G)**

6 Nautical refracting telescope with leather-bound tube, brass draw and inset plate of pendants and flags from the merchant service (**6b**). Further example inset with flags of the world print (**6a**) and a good quality brass eyepiece and draw tube (**6c**). Mid-19th C. 2ft 6in. Each telescope **(C/D)**

7 Stick barometer named after the British hydrographer and meteorologist Admiral Fitzroy. The case is made of ash with gothic-style inspired back panel. 1880s. 3ft. **(C/D)**

8 Traditional Victorian "banjo," or wheel barometer, made in England from rosewood. 19th C. 2ft 10in. **(B/C)**

9 Gould-type microscope made of lacquered brass with a mahogany storage box doubling as stand. The adjustable specimen platform allows the compound lens in the eyepiece (**9a**) to be focused. Mid-19th C. 12in. **(C)**

10 Set of shop balance scales, complete with porcelain slab (**10a**) and brass weights (**10b**). 1860. 2ft 6in high. **(B/C)**

11 French-made opera glasses with telescopic mother-of-pearl handle. 1910. 5½in across. **(B)**

12 Brass sextant for determining latitude and longitude, fitted with small telescope (**12a**) for taking accurate sightings of stars and the sun. Detail (**12b**). 1850s. 8in. **(C/D)**

13 English-made brass refracting telescope in its original case; designed for use on a tripod. Mid-19th C. 2ft 8in. **(D)**

14 Rare pantograph with hinged sections enabling drawings and maps to be copied. Made by Benjamin Martin of Fleet Street, London. Case (**14a**). Mid-18th C. 18in. **(E)**

31a

15 American Edison Gem phonograph with horn and cylindrical record featuring the inventor (**15a**). 1880s. Horn 21in. **(C)**

16 "Ticka Spy Camera" disguised as a pocket watch and made in England from chrome-plated brass (**16a**). 1910. 2½in. **(B)**

17 Mahogany stick barometer with detachable thermometer and ornate mercury reservoir (**17a,b**). Made by the English firm J. B. Dancer. 1840. 3ft 1in. **(E)**

18 Brass balance beam scale with scoop for weighing dry goods. 1870. 20in. **(B)**

19 Military surgeon's kit by J. Weiss & Son. The three metal trays housing the instruments can be immersed in boiling water for easy sterilization. 1917. 2ft. **(C)**

20 Surveyor's dial made of lacquered brass and used for surveying the direction and angle of tunnels. 1880. 10in. **(C)**

21 Mother-of-pearl opera glasses and case, owned by popular English actress Ellen Terry (1847–1928). The maker's name is etched around the eyepieces (**21a**). 1905. 3in. **(C)**

22 Stick barometer with integrated bulb and cistern to store the 30 inches of mercury required. 19th C. 3ft long. **(D)**

23 Ebony and brass octant made by Troughton & Simms of London, in its original oak box. Used by explorers in waters off the North American continent. 1820. 11in. **(C/D)**

24 Georgian ivory draftsman's rule made by Cary of London. Late 18th C. 12in. **(A/B)**

25 Culpeper microscope and protective carrying case. A tray in the base contains accessories. 18th C. 16in. **(C/D)**

26 Precision scale model of a "swift" or industrial machine for winding yarn or thread. Made in Britain. 1900s. 10in. **(D)**

27 Monocular microscope, with six eyepieces of different powers, and other bench accessories. 1880s. 14in. **(C/D)**

28 Leather-bound telescope with Turk's head knot added by the original owner. Late 19th C. 2ft 6in long. **(A)**

29 Versatile chest microscope whose box is also a stand and container for assorted lenses, bone slides (**29a,b**) and specimen receptacles. 1790. 12in. **(D)**

30 Chronometer made in Germany by A. Kittel (**30a**) with a balance to compensate for temperature. 1890. 6in. **(G)**

31 Brass binocular microscope eyepiece. Complete microscope in mahogany case (**31a**). Late 19th C. 15in. **(F)**

PRICE CODE: **A** less than $200 **B** $200–400 **C** $400–750 **D** $750–1,500 **E** $1,500–3,000 **F** $3,000–5,000 **G** over $5,000

TABLES
AND CHAIRS

1 Chippendale, gothic, Federal and Hepplewhite are four classic chair styles. Find a representative of each.

2 Find one table which is not made of wood. What would it have been used for?

3 Name three games associated with tables shown here.

4 Which three tables have links to liquids?

5 Most chairs shown here have a formal character; find two of a more intimate nature.

6 Which piece of furniture has musical associations?

7 What sets 19th-century upholstery apart from that of the previous century?

8 Which chair was made to take outside?

1 Glass-making techniques have created four objects normally associated with other materials: which are they?

2 Glass was decorated in many ways, often adapting techniques from other mediums. Find examples of overlay, cameo and enamel work.

3 Which piece would have been sought-after during the decalcomania craze of the late 19th century?

4 Find an Italian copy of a French original.

5 Two types of popular American glass are "frigger" and "carnival." Find examples and explain their names.

6 Find four styles of early glass made for particular drinks.

7 Which of the five pieces of Tiffany glass is most sought-after?

GLASS

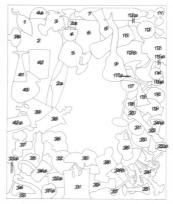

1 Opaque pressed glass perfume bottle molded to resemble a bunch of grapes. 1875. 3in. *(A/B)*

2 Favrile vase by American makers Tiffany with iridescent gold finish. The body tapers to a narrow stem and stand (2a). 1900s. 11in. *(G)*

3 Italian Art Deco lamp in the form of a lemon tree. Each fruit conceals a bulb (3a). Ornamental glass base (3b). 1920s. 14in high. *(B)*

4 Layered glass lampshade made by Müller Frères of the Luneville Glassworks in France. 1900–10. 16in. Table lamp *(F)*

5 Pair of English engraved glasses, known as "rummers," depicting a local feat of civil engineering, the Sunderland Bridge. 1840. 6in. Pair *(C)*

6 Mosaic of sulfur-crested cockatoos on a flowering shrub in iridescent and opaque glass. Attributed to Joseph Briggs of the Tiffany mosaic studio. c.1905. 2ft 7in high. *(G)*

7 Glass rolling pin. The interior is pasted with colourful transfers and sealed with a paint wash. 1880s. 12in. *(C)*

8 Tiffany aquamarine glass vase, with fish, sea urchins and seaweed embedded in green "sea water." 1913. 8in. *(G)*

9 Art Nouveau gooseneck vase by Austrian makers Loetz, using cobalt iridescent "papillon" art glass (a purely decorative glass). 1900. 10in high. *(G)*

10 Loetz vase in amethyst iridescent "papillon" glass with a silver decoration applied by electrolysis. 1900. 8in. *(D/E)*

11 "Fountain dumpies" made in England from waste glass and used as paperweights. 1860s. 5½ and 3½in. Set *(B)*

12 Millefiori mushroom paperweight made in St. Louis, France. Millefiori, "little flowers," are created by melting rods of colored glass together (12a,b). 1848. 2⅜in. *(E)*

13 American glass candy dish. 1890s. 7½in. *(A)*

14 Stopper from a two-color Bohemian ship's decanter. Complete decanter (14a). 1920. 9in. *(A)*

15 Cordial glass with color-twist stem (15a) made by William Beilby of Newcastle, England. 1760–70. 6in. *(E/F)*

16 Iridescent glass dishes with crimped decoration around the rims (16a). 1910–30. 5–6in. *(A)*

17 Wine glass by Otto Prutscher for the Austrian company NEFF with secessionist pattern (17a). 1905. 8in. *(E)*

18 Favrile vase by Tiffany, loosely based on a Turkish rosewater sprinkler and painted with soft gold and peacock blue on a black glass. 1908. 12in. *(F/G)*

19 Pod-shaped Art Nouveau vase in magenta, electric and peacock iridescent blues. Made by Tiffany. 1906. 7in. *(D/E)*

20 Millefiori paperweight made in England. Mid-19th C. 1¼in. *(A)*

21 Cypriotware vase from Tiffany with a pitted, lustrous surface achieved by coating the surface with minute glass chips and lustering with metallic oxides. 1908. 4in. *(G)*

22 Candlestick made by mixing end-of-day colored glass. Detail (22a). 1870s. 8in. *(A)*

23 Small rose design paperweight from either China or Bohemia. 1900s. 1½in. *(A)*

24 Cranberry glass "epergne" or centerpiece with six trumpet-shaped flower holders and two matching vases (24a,b). 1870. 22in. *(D)*

25 Goblet with a folded foot and trumpet-shaped bowl. 1730–40. 8in. *(E)*

26 Claret decanter with attractive rococo-style silver shell and coral shaped mounts. 1882. 10in. *(F)*

27 Working glass trumpet with a drawn and twisted stem; made to show the glassmaker's skill. c.1840. 2ft 1in. *(B/C)*

28 Bust of Emperor Napoleon III (1808–73) made in St. Louis, France. 1873. 8in. *(B/C)*

29 Vase imitating the style of Lalique. c.1920. 8in. *(A)*

30 Condiment set in pressed glass. c.1900. 5in long. *(A)*

31 Clear and frosted glass figurine of "Suzanne" by glass and jewelry designer René Lalique (1860–1945) with bronze illuminated base depicting peacocks. 1930s. 8in. *(G)*

32 Rummer engraved with sailing ships and a message of friendship, with lemon squeezer base (32a). c.1780. 5in. *(C)*

33 Fine press-molded swan-shaped tureen cover and dish (33a). Complete piece (33b). 1910. 8in long. *(A)*

34 Glass lemonade jug and beaker (34a), crafted to resemble cut glass, with design of lilies. 1910–20. 12in. *(A)*

35 Mass-produced pressed glass dish in the shade of orange popular until WWII. 1910. 6in. *(A)*

36 Rare layered glass lampshade made at the Daum Frères glassworks in Nancy, France. 1900. 18in. *(G)*

37 Tiffany lava glass vases which simulate the effect of flowing lava (37a). 1908. 4–8in high. *(G)*

38 Bohemian ruby glass vase and cover, engraved with a woodland scene. 1850. 18in. *(F)*

39 Molded opalescent figurine by the Marius Sabino glassworks in Italy. 1930s. 8in. *(E)*

40 Millefiori vase with trailing foliage and flower heads embedded in the glass. 1902. 8in. *(C)*

41 Drinking glass with typical engraved images of hops and barley, associated with its contents. 1770. 5in. *(A)*

42 German souvenir beaker with view of health spa near Dresden or Leipzig and floral decoration in enamel (42a). 1812. 4in. *(G)*

14a

33b

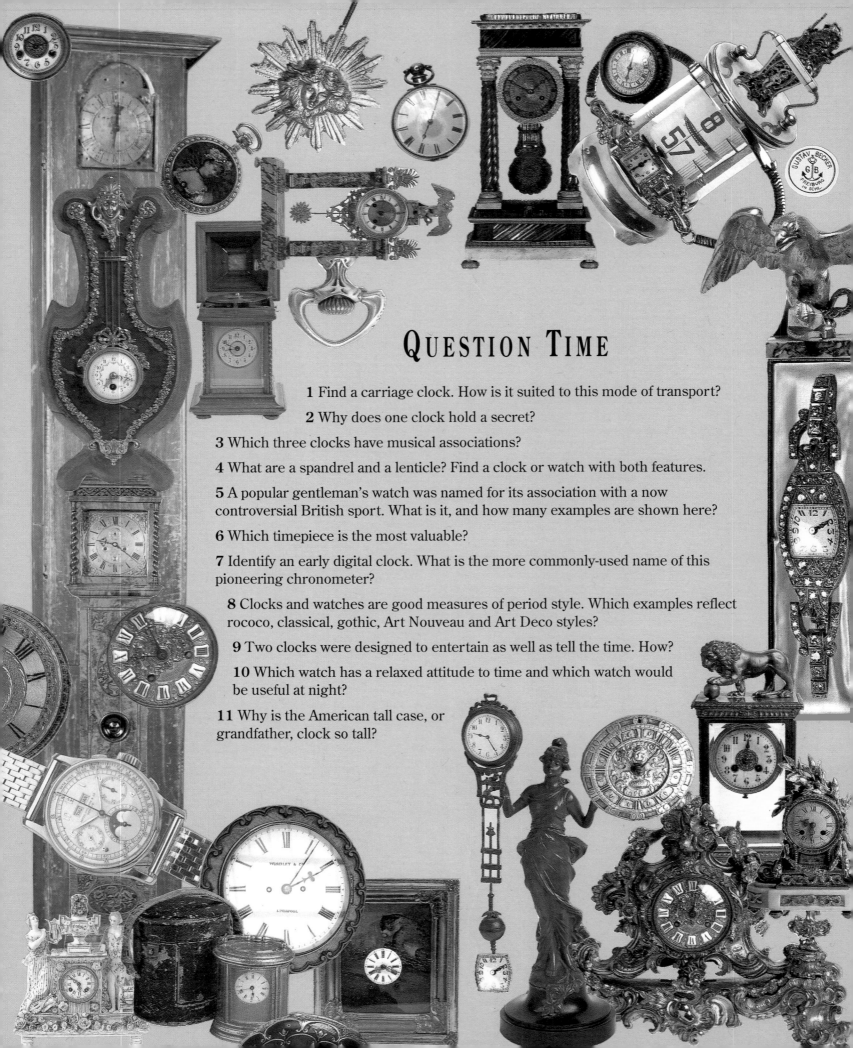

QUESTION TIME

1 Find a carriage clock. How is it suited to this mode of transport?

2 Why does one clock hold a secret?

3 Which three clocks have musical associations?

4 What are a spandrel and a lenticle? Find a clock or watch with both features.

5 A popular gentleman's watch was named for its association with a now controversial British sport. What is it, and how many examples are shown here?

6 Which timepiece is the most valuable?

7 Identify an early digital clock. What is the more commonly-used name of this pioneering chronometer?

8 Clocks and watches are good measures of period style. Which examples reflect rococo, classical, gothic, Art Nouveau and Art Deco styles?

9 Two clocks were designed to entertain as well as tell the time. How?

10 Which watch has a relaxed attitude to time and which watch would be useful at night?

11 Why is the American tall case, or grandfather, clock so tall?

Question Time

1 American tall case clock mounted in a simple painted pine case. The movement and face are English. 1730s. 5ft 8in. **(G)**

2 Enameled gold pocket watch set with split pearls and two minute rose diamonds. Made in Switzerland, probably for the Chinese market. Obverse side **(2a)**. 1890. 1¼in. **(D)**

3 English mantel set consisting of a clock and two candelabras **(3a)** devised to complement Victorian mantelpieces. Fashioned from veined marble with gilt brass figures of Egyptian maidens, eagles **(3b)** and a spagnolette or "sunburst" pendulum bob **(3c)**. 1880. Clock 21in. **(E/F)**

4 Silver pair-cased, or farmer's, verge watch. Made in England, this design **(4a)** was introduced in 1800 and remained popular for the next 60 years. Pair-cased refers to the outer case which gives extra protection. 1825. 2¼in. **(B)**

5 Rare French portico clock (four columns supporting a platform or entablature) made of ribbed blue glass with ormolu mounts. Engraved face **(5a)**. 1840. 2ft. **(G)**

6 Early English watch, with verge escapement, signed by the watchmaker Richard Riccard. The silver dial **(6a)** is engraved with stylized tulips, which also appear as pinwork decoration on the leather case **(6b)**. 1660. 3in. **(G)**

7 Fashionable cocktail watch with diamonds mounted in platinum and a 9ct white gold bracelet. 1935. ¾in face. **(C)**

8 Flick clock made by the German company Junghans. It is visually a forerunner of digital clocks developed later in the century. Tiny pointers hold back the time cards. 1905. 5in. **(C)**

9 Trademark of Gustav Becker from Freiburg, Germany, and found on the movement of the firm's Black Forest mantel clocks.

10 Diamond and platinum bracelet watch with lozenge-shaped dial **(10a)** and stirrup shoulders typical of its period. The maker is unidentified. 1920s. 3in long. **(E/F)**

11 White gold wristwatch made by Audemars Piguet for the Swiss watchmakers Gubelin of Lucerne, with a minute repeating movement unusual in a watch this size. 1930s. 1in. **(G)**

12 English novelty clock carved from wood to appear medieval with gilt face and supports. 1860s. 9in high. **(C)**

13 Full-calendar clock made by the English watchmaker Dent. The cast case, with masks, fruit and scroll work, is very ornate for the mid-19th century. Two of its three subsidiary dials are shown **(13a,b)**. Hands **(13c)**. 1860. 6in. **(E)**

14 Swedish painted tall case clock with moldings picked out in gold leaf. The square dial **(14a)** with arched top is a feature widely found in continental Europe. 1750s. 8ft. **(F)**

15 Gilt face from English bracket clock. Late 19th C. 4in.

16 Early verge watch by the English maker Peter Garon, with engraved dial in chased silver and gilt **(16a)**. An outer case with glass lid keeps out dust **(16b)**. 1690. 2½in. **(E)**

17 American hunter-cased gold watch with a chain and fob made for sale in the English market. 1890. 2¼in. **(D)**

18 Miniature tall case clock made in France. Polished mahogany case with an arched brass dial, inscribed *Tempus fugit* ("Time flies"). 1885. 2ft 2in. **(B/C)**

19 French mantel clock produced for export to Britain. What appears to be marble is in fact steel with gilt decoration. The movement is signed "Marti à Paris," but the dial **(19a)** is by British clockmaker John Bennett. 1880. 17in. **(C)**

20 Striking wall clock from northern England finished in walnut veneer and carved **(20a)**. Hands **(20b)**. 1850. 15in. **(D)**

21 Dial and minute hand **(21a)** from an American eight-day mantel clock by Boston maker W. H. Young. 1850. 19in. **(D)**

22 Elaborate pierced metal mantel clock set. The bombé (bulging) style of the clock case is repeated in the two accompanying vases **(22a,b)**. 1890. 15in. **(C)**

23 Walnut tall case clock with paneled marquetry by Robert

55b

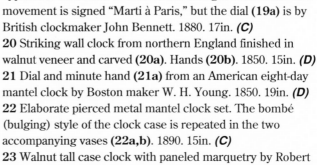

Dingley of London; the original green staining on the marquetry leaves can still be seen. 1690. 6ft 6in. **(G)**

24 Scottish tall case clock by Alexander Nicol of Arbroath. The painted arch shows a battle scene and on the spandrels are representations of the seasons **(24a)**. 1800. 6ft 8in. **(E)**

25 Engraved gold dial from a Swiss pocket watch by "Le Comte" of Geneva with typical Swiss engraving and translucent blue enameled case **(25a)**. The spiral pattern **(25b)** is created on a special lathe. 1875. 1½in. **(C)**

26 Ebony and metal mounted mantel clock by Thwaite and Reid of London, with chiming movement. 1860s. 3ft. **(G)**

27 Single-cased verge watch with a small, or half-hunter, window exposing the inner chapter ring when the lid is closed. Made in England. 1820. 2in. **(B)**

28 London-made gentleman's lever watch in 18ct gold, with a gold balance wheel inside. It has a scrolled double "frame" or cartouche in the center **(28a)**, attractive hallmarked winder **(28c)** and hands **(28b)**. 1877. 1¼in. **(C)**

29 American shelf clock by the New Haven Clock Co. **(29c)** with pressed wood (gingerbread) surround, metal inlaid enamel dial **(29a,b)** and eight-day movement. 1900. 22in. **(B)**

30 Lacquered English wall clock with "drop dial" face **(30a)** and mother-of-pearl inlay. 1860. 2ft. **(C/D)**

31 Dial from a German architectural-style mantel clock made by the Hamburg American Clock Co. 1900. 20in. **(A)**

32 Swiss-made enameled gold watch. When the winder is pressed the repeating mechanism restrikes the preceding hour; rare in a watch of this size. 1890. 1½in. **(F/G)**

33 American architectural shelf clock in ebonized and gilded pine with pointed finials on the hood. 1885. 19in. **(A)**

34 English mahogany teardrop shaped wall clock signed by the maker Jno (John) Nevil of Norwich. 1790. 4ft 2in. **(G)**

35 Victorian tall case clock in a light oak case signed Gaze Ebrors, London. An allegorical Father Time is depicted on the partly gold ground. 19th C. 8ft 2in. **(E/F)**

36 Long pendulum wall clock by the London clockmaker Richard Hindmore, decorated with chinoiserie on the case. 1725. 5ft 9in **(G)**

37 George III mahogany tall case clock by Conyers Dunlop of London. The top dial can be set to strike or silent **(37a)**. Detail of main dial **(37b)**. 1770. 7ft. **(F/G)**

38 Elegant wall clock with mahogany frame and heart-shaped hour hand **(38a)**; made in England and signed Penney of Cambridge. 1875. 15in. **(C)**

39 Dial with roman numerals from a classic American shelf clock. 1895. 6in.

40 Hexagonal wall clock which strikes the hours on a bell. Signed on face **(40a)** by Thomas of Lincoln. 1870. 16in. **(E)**

41 English silver pair-cased pocket watch. The dial **(41a)** is decorated with a frigate and, instead of numbers, bears the owner's name: Thomas Baldwin. Details of winder **(41b)**, hands **(41c)**. 1793. 2¼in. **(E)**

42 Steel mantel clock, transfer-printed to resemble slate or marble. Mass-produced in the United States for export overseas. 1879. 18in. **(A)**

43 Watchstand made by American whalers from bone and marine ivory, known as scrimshaw, and enclosed in a wooden frame. 1833. 2ft. **(E)**

44 Louis XVI-style striking mantel clock in marble and ormolu. 19th-century revival items closely resembled their 18th-century originals. 1850s. 12in. **(D/E)**

45 "Four glass" clock – all four sides are glass – made in Germany's Black Forest. The lion and base are not brass, but spelter, an alloy of zinc. 1895. 16in. **(A/B)**

46 French gilt-brass mantel clock in a blend of earlier Louis XV and XVI styles forming a hybrid shape that never existed in the 18th century. Dial **(46a)**. 1875. 15in. **(D)**

47 Bronzed soft metal clock made in France; the clock **(47a)** and pendulum are held aloft by a figurine. 1900–10. 12in. **(B)**

48 German picture clock with an eight-day movement by the well-known clockmaker Sattele Eisenbach. The face is protected by a glass-mounted frame. 1860. 12in. **(E/F)**

49 Miniature oval carriage clock with fitted case made in France by A. Dumas. 1870. 4in. **(C)**

50 Ceramic mantel clock handmade in Dresden with two Grecian figures representing the arts. Late 19th C. 15in. **(E)**

51 Gold chronograph made by Patek Philippe & Co., with stopwatch, perpetual calendar and day, month and phases of the moon. 1945. Dial 1¼in. **(G)**

52 Tall case clock signed by the English clockmaker Daniel Smith. The case is walnut inlaid with floral marquetry; a glass lenticle exposes the pendulum. 1720. 8ft 2in. **(F/G)**

53 Lyre-shaped clock from France with red marble and ormolu case, backed by a velour mount. 1900. 16in. **(C)**

54 Novelty mantel clock in oak, with a musical movement made by the British company Symphonion. 1900. 10in. **(C)**

55 Winder and hands **(55a)** in Art Nouveau style from a silver-plated motoring watch **(55b)**. 1910. **(C/D)**

56 Face from a German "faux marbre" (fake marble) wooden mantel clock. 1890. 5in.

24a

PRICE CODE: **A** less than $200 **B** $200–400 **C** $400–750 **D** $750–1,500 **E** $1,500–3,000 **F** $3,000–5,000 **G** over $5,000

31

CHINA CLOSET

1 Find four teapots disguised as: a building, metal, flora and fauna and wickerwork.

2 China decoration takes many forms. Find something painted, printed, plated and pierced.

3 Find pieces associated with seafood, lighting, drinking coffee and drugs.

4 Find pieces purporting to be ancient Egyptian, classical, Renaissance and rococo.

5 Which pieces have theatrical, literary and film associations?

6 Which pieces depict travel by land, sea and air?

7 Find examples of salt glaze, parian ware and slipware.

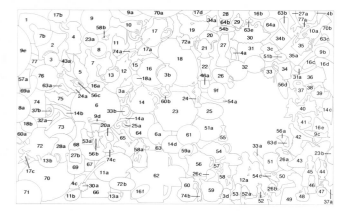

1 Wemyssware dressing-table tray. 1905. 11in. **(C/D)**

2 Wemyssware egg basket. 1910. 8in. **(C/D)**

3 One of two Doulton jugs advertising Dewar's whisky **(3b)**. Other jug **(3a)**. Called "Rembrandtware" after the portraits **(3c,d)** which mimic the artist's style. 1910–20. 7in. Each **(B)**

4 German Toby jug of a town crier **(4a,b)** ringing his bell and wearing the traditional tricorne hat **(4c)**. 1890. 8in. **(A)**

5 Unusual Mason's Ironstone vases gilded and painted in the Japanese Imari style. 1830s. 2ft 4in high. Pair **(E)**

6 Worcester plate with family crest **(6a)**. 1813. 9¼in. **(E)**

7 Worcester sweetmeat figures. 1865. 8in high. **(D)**

8 Meissen gloss-gilded plate. The intricate pattern **(8a)** was painted on in liquid gold. 1840s. 11in. **(B)**

9 Poole pottery plate commemorating the landing in Poole Harbor of the Empire Airways flying boat. The designer's and painter's names appear on the back **(9f)**. Details **(9a–e)**. 1940. 15in. **(E)**

10 Pair of neoclassical Dresden vases based on an 1815 design. Late 19th C. 16in. **(E/F)**

11 Painted and gilded Worcester sauce tureen with lid **(11a)** and ladle **(11b)**. 1775. 7in. **(E)**

12 Art Nouveau piece from Royal Dux, Bohemia. The molding of the nymphs' faces **(12a)** is of high quality. c.1900. 16in. **(C)**

13 Wedgwood silver-plated earthenware sugar bowl, milk jug **(13a)** and teapot **(13b)**. 1900.

57b Teapot 4in. Set **(B)**

14 Early Meissen teapot, with scrolled handle **(14a)** and curved gilded spout **(14b)**. The pot's enameled lid is also gilded **(14c,d)**. 1723. 5in. **(G)**

15 Pre-Columbian whistling pot from Peru. c.1300. 9in. **(A)**

16 Minton soup plate, covered dish **(16a)**, dinner plates **(16b,c)**, fruit bowl **(16d,e)** and large dish **(16f)** in an oriental pattern. 1805. Dinner plate 10in. Each **(A)**

17 Meissen chocolate pot and cover in the Japanese Arita style **(17c)**. The lid **(17a,b)** has a hole through which to stir the chocolate and a gold rim **(17d)**. 1740s. 8in. **(E)**

18 Worcester taper or candlestick painted in a Japanese "finger and thumb" pattern **(18a)** with the Chamberlains mark **(18b)**. 1800–1805. 4in wide. **(B)**

19 English earthenware crowned lion on base, probably painted by child workers. c.1780. 4½in. **(D)**

20 Lid for a Belleek basket; unusual delicately colored flowers **(20a)** add to the value. 1880. 10in. Basket **(F)**

21 Cabbage teapot with a snake forming handle and spout; revival of French 17th-century style. Late 19th C. 7in. **(A/B)**

22 Majolica conservatory seat modeled as a winged harpy with lion's legs. c.1875. 17in. **(E)**

23 Minton's majolica dish, meant for oysters as the fish design **(23b)** shows. Sauce dish **(23a)**. 1889. 11in. **(B)**

24 Meissen statuettes of *Commedia dell'Arte* figures by craftsman Peter Reinicke. Figure **(24a)**. 1743. 7in. **(E)**

25 Chelsea porcelain plate, painted with vegetables, insects and a butterfly typical of the makers **(25a)**. c.1755. 9in. **(D)**

26 English pink and yellow vase in antique Greek style. Details of top **(26b,c)**. Other vase **(26a)**. 1860. 6in. Pair **(B)**

27 Martinware stoneware bird, with outsize clawed feet **(27a)** and detachable head **(27b)**. London. 1898. 11in. **(G)**

28 Meissen plate with gloss-gilding **(28a)**. 1840s. 11in. **(B)**

57b

59b

29 Monkey's head cover for a Minton majolica teapot **(29a)**. 1890. 5in. **(C)**

30 Belleek basket with perfectly formed flowers **(30a)** and handles and feet imitating coral. 1904. 11in. **(D)**

31 Detachable beaker, made to resemble an owl's head, from a Staffordshire slipware jug. Detail of the eye **(31a)**. 17th C. 3in high. Jug **(G)**

32 Two of six pearlware plates made in Yorkshire and decorated with painted birds **(32a)**. c.1820. 8in. Set **(E)**

33 Miniature creamware teapot, part of a child's tea set. Details show the spout **(33a)** and the painted flowers **(33b)**. c.1810. 4in high. **(B/C)**

34 Napoleon-style cup based on a Sèvres original. Detail of the foot **(34a)**. Painted mark **(34b)**. 1900. 3½in high. **(B)**

35 Saltglaze teapot by John and Thomas Wedgwood in the shape of the Big House at Burslem **(35a)**. 1750. 5in high. **(E)**

36 *Maiolica* jar from Palermo, Sicily. The picture of St. Lucy carrying eyes on a plate indicates the jar was meant for eye ointment **(36a)**. c.1580. 12in. **(F/G)**

37 Minton's majolica novelty teapot; the hen's head **(37a)** forms the spout, and its tail **(37b)** the handle. 1872. 8in. **(C/D)**

38 Meissen mark used during the 1840s.

39 Belleek mark for the period 1891–1926.

40 Rare Coalport copy of a domestic scene taken from the German makers Meissen. c.1840. 10in. **(E)**

41 One of a pair of Staffordshire painted pottery zebras. 1850. 8½in high. Pair **(C)**

42 Canary from Bow, London. 1760. 3in. Pair **(E)**

43 Realistic china court shoe by Royal Worcester with gilt "seeding" **(43a)**. 1919. 7¾in long. **(G)**

36a

44 Royal Crown Derby jug. 1900. 10in high. **(B)**

45 Very rare naive Staffordshire saltglazed stoneware figure of a bell lady. 1740. 4in high. **(G)**

46 The Cheshire cat, from a rare series of Royal Worcester *Alice in Wonderland* figures. Detail **(46a)**. 1950s. 3in. **(D)**

47 Date mark from French makers Sèvres for the year 1880.

48 French faience figure of a girl with baskets, probably used for holding salt at table. 1790. 8in. **(E)**

49 Very rare Rockingham dog. 1830. 4in long. **(D)**

50 Belleek earthenware bedpan. 1870–80. 10in. **(A)**

51 Derby yellow-ground "cabinet" cup and saucer **(51a)** decorated with painted scenes **(51b)**. c.1790. 3in. **(C)**

52 Walt Disney pottery characters **(52a)** from *The Lady and the Tramp*. 1950s. 5–6in. Each **(A/B)**

53 One of a pair of Staffordshire spaniels modeled on more expensive porcelain. Other spaniel **(53a)**. 1850. 11in. **(B/C)**

54 Irish Belleek teapot, cup and saucer and cake plate **(54a)** in the Shamrock pattern; detail of the inside of the cup **(54b)** and the teapot lid **(54c)**. 1895. Plate 6½in. Set **(D/E)**

55 Stoneware Tinworth mouse menu-holder. c.1885. 4in. **(D)**

56 Mabel Lucie Attwell teapot with transfer-printed outline and hand coloring **(56c)**. The orange spout **(56a)**, handle and knop **(56d)**, and kewpie figure **(56b)** are typical of the period. 1925. 5in. **(A)**

57 Decorative detail and band **(57a)** from an unusual earthenware ewer made by Bishop and Stonier in England. Complete ewer **(57b)**. 1875. 13½in high. **(C)**

58 Front and back view **(58a)** of a painted Staffordshire figure of a huntsman. Detail **(58b)**. c.1850. 12in. **(B)**

59 Art Deco teapot and sugar bowl from a breakfast set **(59b)**. Detail of geometric design **(59a)**. 1930. Teapot 4in. Set **(B)**

60 One of two Mason's Ironstone octagonal jugs. Other jug **(60a)**. Green dragon handle **(60b)**. c.1840. 10in. **(A)**

61 Vienna-style cabinet plate with portrait. 1890. 9in. **(C)**

62 Clarice Cliff Art Deco tea service in "Bizarre" design. 1930s. Teapot 5in high. Set for six **(D/E)**

63 Clarice Cliff mustard pot and lid **(63e)**, pepper **(63a,b)** and salt shakers **(63c,d)**. 1930s. 3½in high. **(B)**

64 Imari-type pattern Worcester dessert plate with "gothic" oak leaves **(64a)**. Detail of center **(64b)**. 1808. 8in. **(B)**

65 Mantelpiece ornament by German makers Sitzendorf, probably used for holding spills. 1890. 10in high. **(A)**

66 Original maker's mark for Mason's Ironstone.

67 Maker's mark for Royal Worcester. c.1910.

68 Pair of Dutch porcelain vases from the Oude Loosdrecht factory following a popular Meissen style. 1770s. 7in. **(E)**

69 Rockingham porcelain mug, with typical rococo-style gilded decoration **(69a)**. c.1835. 4in. **(D)**

70 Nymphenburg plate painted with flowers and insects **(70a,b)** by Josef Zachenberger. c.1760. 9in. **(G)**

71 Armorial-style dish made in China. 1730. 9in. **(D)**

72 Typical Sunderland ewer and basin printed with verses **(72a)** and local views **(72b)**. c.1840. Bowl 12in; jug 9in. **(C)**

73 Rare 19th-century white Sèvres vase with Art Nouveau style decoration in enamels and gilding. 1881. 5¼in. **(C/D)**

74 Stacey Marks Minton tile panel with falconry scene in Art Nouveau style. Details **(74a–c)**. 1871. 12in. **(C)**

75 Irish Belleek parian crouching Venus. Late 19th C. 17in. **(G)**

76 Copy of a 16th-century Italian *maiolica* charger from the Della Robbia factory at Birkenhead. 1894. 12in. **(E)**

77 Wedgwood majolica bowl with silver-plated mount in the popular fan pattern with birds **(77a)**. 1879. 10in. **(C)**

29a

PRICE CODE: **A** less than $200 **B** $200–400 **C** $400–750 **D** $750–1,500 **E** $1,500–3,000 **F** $3,000–5,000 **G** over $5,000

35

WHATNOTS TO WARDROBES

1 Stringing and cross-banding are types of decoration. Where would you find them?

2 Find three pieces of furniture with links to literature.

3 Gilded bronze mounts are a feature of furniture made in which country? What is this type of metal called?

4 Furniture decoration need not be of wood; find examples of painting, ivory and three types of metal.

5 Locate a whatnot, a credenza and a linen press. What were they used for?

6 The piano stool (9) is designated "Federal"; where and what period is it from?

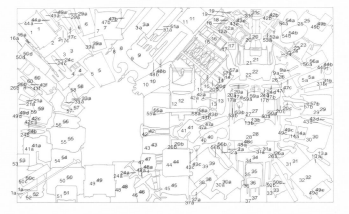

19a

17d

1 *Secrétaire à abattant* with figured mahogany grain, made in Altona, Denmark. Turned column and carved foot (1a). 1840. 4ft 10in. **(E)**

2 Victorian stool with scrolled rosewood legs (2a). c.1850. 2ft 6in x 4ft. **(F)**

3 English satinwood cabinet with hand-painted panel surrounded by ebony border (3a). 19th C. 4ft. **(G)**

4 Sheraton revival sideboard. Early 20th C. 4ft 6in long. **(D)**

5 Art Deco sycamore sideboard by French designer Jacques Adnet. It is banded in stainless steel with glass panels covering the top (5a). 1925–30. 7ft long. **(G)**

6 Early Victorian glazed-door cabinet in mahogany with cupboards and a drawer. 1845. 8ft. **(F)**

7 Danish walnut veneered "commode," or chest of drawers, with gilt detailing and rococo-style handles. The wooden top is painted to resemble marble. 1775–1800. 2ft 9in. **(G)**

8 Mahogany six-shell desk and bookcase made by American cabinet maker John Goddard. 1760–70. 10ft 10in. **(G)**

9 Federal mahogany piano stool with reeded legs (9a) and base. Made in New York. c.1800–10. 2ft 6in. **(F/G)**

10 Maltese secretaire-bookcase with olivewood and walnut veneering and scrolling cornice. 1780. 6ft. **(G)**

11 Secret compartment from a secretaire-bookcase. A catch within the small cupboard releases the hollow right-hand pillar. Secretaire-bookcase (11a). 1730s. 6ft 5in. **(G)**

12 Italian cabinet veneered in ebony with ivory marquetry. The central panels are engraved with classical scenes in Renaissance style (12a). 19th C. 5ft 6in high. **(F)**

13 English walnut writing table with built-in writing box (13a). The simple table top (13b) and ornately carved legs reflect the eclectic style of the Victorians. 1840s. 3ft 6in. **(F)**

14 George III mahogany buffet or sideboard from England with bowed top and tulipwood cross-banding on the drawer and doors (14a). 1790. 4ft 2in long. **(G)**

15 Cast-iron and brass bedstead with looped design. 1870. 4ft 6in wide. **(D)**

16 Four-tier whatnot with spiral-turned columns (16a). 1870. 6ft high. **(D)**

17 "Perspective" panel in handcut veneers from a 17th-century oak chest (17d). Drawer fronts (17a–c). 1660. 3ft high. **(G)**

18 Full-sized cheval, or four-legged, glass in mahogany with original brass candle holders. 1820–30. 6ft 6in. **(D/E)**

19 Rococo drawer handle in gilt from a Swedish chest of drawers. (19a). 1775–1800. 2ft 8in high. **(G)**

20 Mahogany wig stand. A circular frame supports a bowl for powdering wigs (20a) and drawers beneath (20b) hold the necessary materials. Detail of foot (20c) and carved vertical support (20d). 1755–60. 2ft 7in high. **(F)**

21 Dutch walnut roll-top desk, with diamond parquetry on the roll top and cross-banding around the drawers (21a) and top. 1780s. 3ft 7in high. **(F/G)**

22 Lady's writing desk, or *bonheur du jour*, in the mixture of French styles known as *tous les Louis*. Made from burr walnut, with kingwood cross-banding. 1860. 3ft 7in wide. **(F)**

23 Chippendale-style cheval glass. 1900. 6ft high. **(E)**

24 Mahogany three-tiered dumbwaiter, one of a pair (24a). Food was left on the trays so that guests could help themselves. c.1775–85. 4ft. Pair **(G)**

25 Miniature mahogany chest with stud feet and elegant shaped apron beneath bottom drawer. 18th C. 12in high. **(B)**

26 Doll's-house sofa upholstered in olive silk (26b) on a stained wooden frame (26a). 1890. 9in long. **(A)**

27 Georgian mahogany corner cupboard with bow front and brass fittings. Made in England. 1780s. 4ft high. **(D/E)**

28 Painted dressing table with gilt mounts and fabric apron. Made in the United States. Late 18th C. 3ft. **(G)**

29 English George II writing desk with highly figured

PRICE CODE: **A** less than $200 **B** $200–400 **C** $400–750 **D** $750–1,500 **E** $1,500–3,000 **F** $3,000–5,000 **G** over $5,000

walnut veneer exterior showing off the grain, and oak drawer linings. Front of drawer with fittings **(29a)**. 1735. 3ft high. **(G)**

30 Burr walnut davenport desk. Side drawers provide space for personal possessions and documents **(30a)**. 1870. 2ft wide. **(G)**

31 Mahogany writing desk with sloping fall-front decorated with marquetry panel **(31a)** and boxwood lines on drawer fronts **(31b)**. Interior door panel **(31c)**. 1780. 3ft 6in. **(E)**

32 Miniature English chest of drawers in oyster veneer with marquetry inlay and button handles. 1790s. 14in high. **(C)**

33 French Louis XV-style bedstead in walnut with beading and carved footboard **(33a)**. 1895. 4ft 6in wide. **(E)**

34 American Hepplewhite-style card table made from mahogany with green baise surface. *c.*1790–1810. 3ft high. **(G)**

35 Bedside commode with false drawer fronts concealing a chamber pot compartment. In Britain the term "commode" can also refer to a chest of drawers. 1778. 2ft 8in high. **(D)**

36 Washstand, or dressing chest, in Hepplewhite style with fold-over top which opens out to provide tray spaces, a mirror and useful compartments. 1800. 2ft 10in. **(E)**

37 Serpentine-shaped chest of drawers from Malta decorated all over with fine marquetry inlays and applied veneer parquetry **(37a)**. 1775–1800. 5ft. **(G)**

38 English Edwardian oak bedstead with typically elegant and restrained carving. 1910. 4ft 7in wide. **(C)**

39 Housekeeper's cupboard in oak with cross-banding on the drawers and fitted clock **(39a)**. 1820. 6ft 6in. **(C/D)**

40 George III mahogany wine cooler with a lead-lined interior for holding ice. 1770. 2ft 2in high. **(G)**

41 Child's kneehole writing desk with leather writing slope and desktop furniture **(41a)**. Mid-19th C. 23in x 22in. **(G)**

42 Triangular mahogany washstand or wig stand designed to fit into a corner. It has three scrolling legs **(42a)**, drawers **(42b)** and a bowl holder **(42c)**. 1765. 2ft 7in. **(E)**

43 Secretaire-bookcase made from mahogany in 18th-century revival style with authentic period detailing **(43a,d,f)** and outstanding glass front **(43b,c,e)**. 1920. 6ft 10in high. **(F)**

44 William and Mary laburnum chest of drawers. The "oyster" veneer is cut across the grain to resemble an oyster shell, hence its name **(44a)**. Turned ball foot **(44b)**. 17th C. 3ft 4in. **(G)**

45 Bow-fronted mahogany chest of drawers with splay feet. 1800–10. 3ft 3in high. **(D)**

46 French-style chest of drawers, with gilded mounts. 19th C. 3ft high. **(G)**

47 Large Hepplewhite-period wine cooler

11a

with brass bands and handles **(47b)**. The four tapering square legs have castors **(47c)**. Lid **(47a)**. 1770. 2ft 4in. **(G)**

48 Inked-in burr walnut writing slope with original inkwell, leather-covered tinder boxes with gilt-metal lids (used to light candles for melting sealing wax), agate quill holder and gilt-metal paperknife **(48b)**. Closed box with cylindrical lid **(48a)** and open leather writing surface **(48c)**. 1850s. 18in. **(D)**

49 18th-century or classical revival cabinet in rosewood decorated with marquetry panels **(49e)**. The edges of the mirrors and cabinet doors have beveled or sloping glass **(49a–d)**. Late 19th C. 6ft 2in high. **(D)**

50 Fine walnut credenza, with high-quality figured veneers and a gilded plaque **(50a,c)** and mounts **(50b)**. It has quarter-circle ends **(50d)** and a single door. 1860. 3ft 7in. **(G)**

51 French revival roll-top desk, based on a 1760s design, with marquetry and gilded mounts **(51a)**. It takes its name from the slatted pull-down cover. 1900–20. 3ft 7in. **(E)**

52 Scottish mahogany pedestal sideboard. The table frieze is banded with brass and fitted with three drawers, flanked by a pair of pedestals on turned feet. 1825. 8ft 4in long. **(G)**

53 Cupboard door from an Arts and Crafts-style dresser **(53c)**. This movement promoted handcrafted rather than machine made furniture; shown in the heavy paneling **(53a)** and large metal mounts **(53b)**. 1910–20. 5ft 6in high. **(F)**

54 Linen press in veneered mahogany with flame mahogany oval panels bordered with satinwood cross-banding and ebonized border **(54a,b)**. 1800–10. 10ft. **(F)**

55 Cylinder-fall davenport in burr walnut. On top is a lockable stationery box and below, framed by turned columns **(55a)**, are shelves to hold music. 1865. 3ft. **(F)**

56 Double-domed secretaire-bookcase from Malta. The bookshelves are glass-fronted **(56a)** and the bureau drawers attractively veneered and inlaid **(56b)**. 1790. 6ft 3in. **(G)**

57 French *lit en bateau*, boat-shaped daybed, made of mahogany in the Empire style. The plain side was pushed against the wall. Splayed leg **(57a,b)**. 1850. 3ft wide. **(D/E)**

58 Louis XV-style bedstead from France with canework panels. A rococo-style garland motif decorates the footboard **(58a)**. 1895. 4ft 6in wide. **(F)**

59 Military-style writing slope in polished mahogany with flush-fitting handles **(59a)**. 1850s. 21in wide. **(D)**

60 Revival glass display case with Chinese Chippendale-style fretting on the cornice and a Sheraton-inspired cabinet and legs. 1900. 6ft 2in. **(D)**

53c

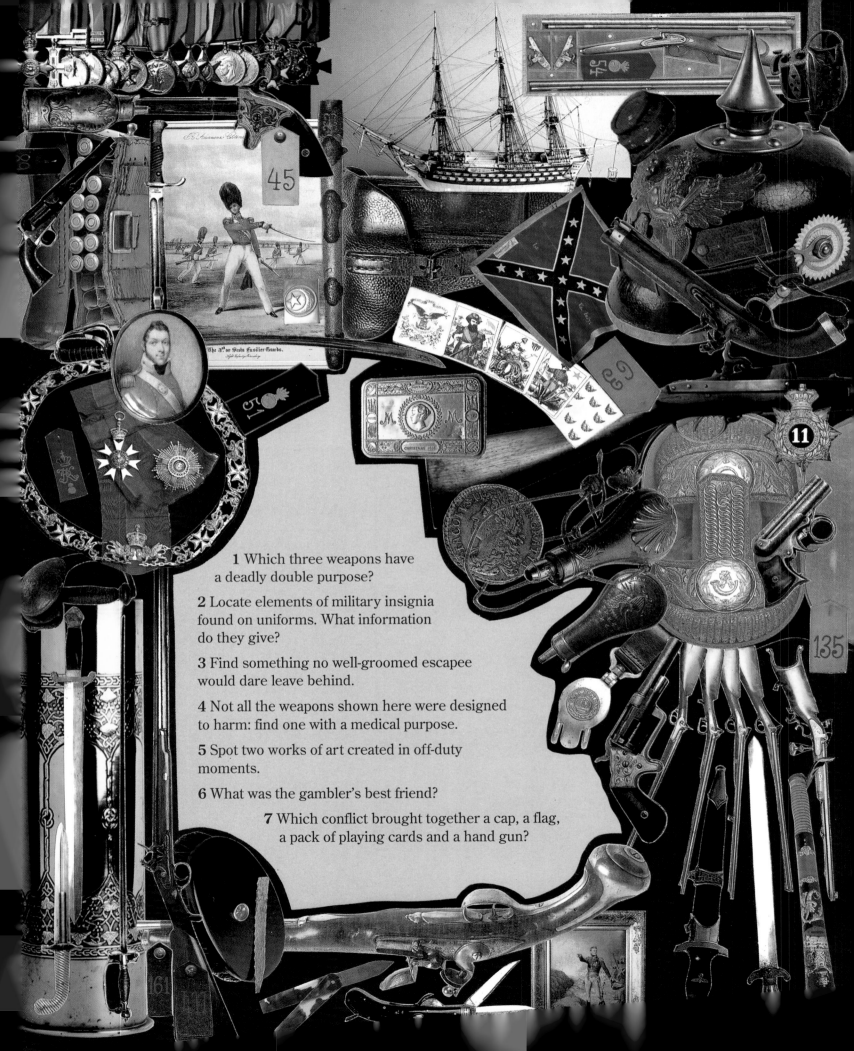

1 Which three weapons have a deadly double purpose?

2 Locate elements of military insignia found on uniforms. What information do they give?

3 Find something no well-groomed escapee would dare leave behind.

4 Not all the weapons shown here were designed to harm: find one with a medical purpose.

5 Spot two works of art created in off-duty moments.

6 What was the gambler's best friend?

7 Which conflict brought together a cap, a flag, a pack of playing cards and a hand gun?

CALL TO ARMS

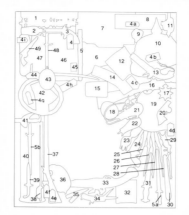

1 Medals awarded to British officer Lt. Col. E. C. Maxwell, dating from the Boer War to WWII. 1904–45. **(B)**

2 English gun flask containing powder, bullets and percussion caps. 1840. 5in. **(A)**

3 Wheelan's patent rimfire pistol with rotating double barrel, used as a concealed weapon. Made in the U.S.A. 1867. 5in. **(B)**

4 Shoulder flashes **(4a–i)** from the Imperial German Army and Navy. 1870–1919. **(A)**

5 Scabbard of dyed and polished sharkskin (shagreen) accommodating a pair of Chinese shortswords **(5a,b)**. 1850. 23in. **(A)**

6 Leather holster for a German Mauser pistol. 1914. 7in. **(A)**

7 Contemporary scale-model of the French three-decker warship *Le Lion,* sporting 100 guns. 1792–1815. 3ft 4in. **(D)**

8 Rare German Stoermer-Herzberg percussion gun, with interchangeable shotgun and rifle barrels. 1830. 3ft 9in. **(F)**

9 Standard-issue Confederate cap or "kepi." 1861–65. **(C)**

10 Spiked helmet or "Pickelhaube" with cockade worn by German soldiers until the end of WWI. 1900. 9in. **(C)**

11 Basket-hilt of a Scottish backsword, probably made for a Highland Militia Regiment. 1740. 3ft 9in. **(C/D)**

12 Confederate battle flag used in the Civil War; replaced the earlier "Stars and Bars" of the South. 1865. **(D)**

13 Holster pistol issued to troops serving the East India Co., a British, Far East-based trading concern. 1840. 15in. **(C)**

14 Patriotic playing cards from the Civil War. 1864. **(B)**

15 Christmas gift, containing tobacco, sent to WWI British servicemen by Princess Mary. 1914. 6in long. **(A)**

16 Hall's Patent Rifle, made in the U.S.A. Breechblock and lock can be removed for use as a pistol. 1831. 3ft 11in. **(D)**

17 British officer's gilt helmet plate from the 11th (North Devon) Regiment. 1878. 2in. **(B)**

18 "Gun money" coin minted by the former British monarch James II (1633–1701), who was forced to melt down his cannon to pay his Irish troops. 1689. 1½in. **(A)**

19 Silver lace "wing" epaulettes worn by a British officer of the 5th Royal Lancashire Militia. 1840s. 7in. **(B)**

20 Remington Derringer pistol with a ring-grip trigger and four barrels; made in the U.S.A. 1866. 4in. **(B)**

21 Gun-metal powder flask with brass fittings made by Flask Co. of Meriden, Connecticut. 1850. 7in. **(A)**

22 Lacquered brass powder flask embossed with the American eagle. 1860s. 4in. **(B)**

23 Rare German Telegraphist's belt buckle from WWI with a drum attachment. 1915. **(A)**

24 Slocum's 320 rimfire patent revolver with sliding tubes and chambers; made in the U.S.A. 1863. 5in. **(C)**

25 English shotgun made by Moore & Woodward. 1840. 3ft 6in. **(D)**

26 Double-barreled shotgun made by the English firm Blanch. 1840. 3ft 10in. **(E)**

27 Shotgun manufactured by the English gunmakers Rigby. 1840. 3ft 10in. **(E)**

28 Belgian shotgun by makers Lassence-Rong. 1840. 3ft 10in. **(D)**

29 Target-shooting gun by Swiss gunsmith Paul. 1840. 3ft 11in. **(D)**

30 Decorated boxwood truncheon bearing the British Crown's insignia. 1815. 12in. **(A)**

31 German presentation dagger issued to officers of the elite SS (*Schutzstaffel*). 1939–45. 14in. **(D)**

32 Portrait of Lt. Col. Sir Robert Harvey painted by Thomas Heaphy (1775–1835). 1815. 23 x 26in. **(E)**

33 Dragoon holster pistol made in England with brass buttcap or "skull crusher" for bludgeoning. 1741. 12in. **(E)**

34 Unwin & Rogers rimfire knife pistol. 1870. 7in folded. **(C)**

35 Pocket fleam with tortoiseshell handles. 1850s. 5in. **(A)**

36 Hairbrush from WWII, with concealed map compass and hacksaw blade. 1940. 4in. **(B)**

37 English Flintlock sporting gun made by William Ryan & Son in Birmingham. 1825. 4ft 2in. **(E)**

38 Scottish small sword with silver hilt inscribed: "Carried for his Prince by Patrick Fea of Airie 1746" **(38a)**. 3ft. **(E)**

39 Lethal knife-pistol made in France; the gun barrel is concealed by a stiletto blade. 1860. 8in. **(B)**

40 Shell case with intricate decoration. 1914–18. 11in. **(B)**

41 Spanish sword with "bilboe" hilt, named after the city of Bilbao where the design originated. 1770. 3ft 4in. **(B)**

42 Regalia of a Knight Grand Cross of the British Order of St. Michael and St. George. 19th C. **(F)**

43 Miniature portrait of an officer painted on ivory as a keepsake. 1820. 3in. **(C)**

44 Hilt of an Indian Army saber, probably issued to a detachment of Mountain Artillery. 1915. 3ft. **(B)**

45 WWI Turkish soldier's belt buckle. 1915. 3in across. **(A)**

46 Ackermann print of Scots Fusilier Guards officer from "Costumes of the British Army." 1820. 10in. **(A)**

47 German cartridge pouch made for Mauser rifle cartridges. 1888. 8in. **(A)**

48 WWI German bayonet, with serrated back. 1912. 14½in long. **(A)**

49 Colt New Army pistol from the Civil War. 1864. 9in. **(E)**

38a

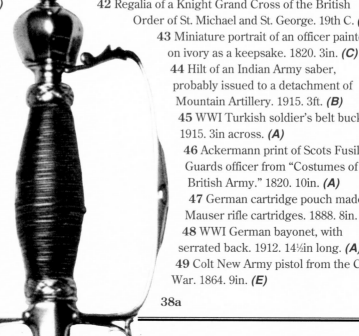

PRICE CODE: **A** less than $200 **B** $200–400 **C** $400–750 **D** $750–1,500 **E** $1,500–3,000 **F** $3,000–5,000 **G** over $5,000

GOLD, SILVER, BRONZE

1 Metalwork is decorated using a variety of techniques. Find a single item with examples of chasing, casting, repousée and engraving.

2 How would you use a quaich, a vinaigrette and an epergne?

3 Find objects useful for the nursery, the smoker and for the bedroom.

4 Name the style period of the following articles: candlestick (36), jug (47) and tea set (71).

5 One piece shown is especially valuable; which is it?

6 Which item is permanently outdoors?

7 How many different metals are represented here?

GOLD, SILVER, BRONZE

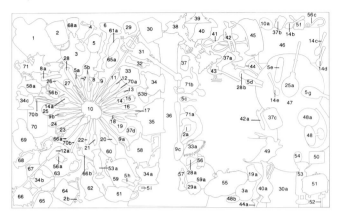

1 Silver hip flask, made in Sheffield. 1929. 6in. *(A)*

2 Copper and brass portable heater, with floral relief pattern **(2a)**; perhaps Middle Eastern. 19th C. 18in high. *(B/C)*

3 Scottish silver quaich commemorating a marriage, and the bride's posy ring **(3a)**. 1654. Quaich 7in. Set *(E)*

4 English bronze of David about to slay Goliath, showing the influence of Rodin. 1895. 11in. *(F/G)*

5 Silver dressing-table set with tray and buttonhook; clothes brushes **(5a,e,h)**; cuticle shaper **(5b)**; hairbrushes **(5c,d,g)**; hand mirror **(5f)**; and cosmetic jars **(5i)**, decorated in romantic fashion. 1900. Mirror 12in long. *(D)*

6 One of a pair of cast-silver candlesticks in typical mid-18th-century design. Late 19th C. 10in. Pair *(F)*

7 Bone-handled butter knife, Birmingham. 1834. 6in. *(A)*

8 Baby's gold rattle with bells, a whistle and a coral teether **(8a)**. Made in London. 1860. 7in long. *(G)*

9 French silver dessert spoon with patterned back **(9a)**, fork **(9b)** and serving spoon **(9c)** from set of 12. 1724. 8in. Set *(G)*

10 George III silver punch ladle with a beaded edge to the bowl **(10a)** and twisted whalebone handle. 1780. 14in. *(B)*

11 Silver fiddle-pattern butter knife with milkmaid engraving. Hyam Hyams, London. 1869. 8in. *(A)*

12 Butter knife with silver blade and stained ivory handle by John Daly of Dublin. Detail **(12a)**. 1795. 8½in. *(A)*

13 Broad-bladed butter knife with ivory handle. Made in France. 1820. 7½in. *(A)*

14 Silver egg spoon with gilded bowl and Lewis Carroll-type figure on the handles. One of a set of six **(14a–e)**. 1890. 4½in. One spoon *(C)*

15 Silver match case with a ridged striker. Late 19th C. 1½in. *(A)*

16 Silver butter knife in palm pattern by George Adams, London. 1878. 8in. *(A)*

17 Butter knife with silver-gilt blade and polished horn handle. 1809. 9in. *(A)*

18 Bone-handled butter knife. 1813. 5in. *(A)*

19 Swedish silver beaker with stylized flower work and plain silver beaker **(19a)**. 1726 and 1735. Both 3½in. Each *(C)*

20 Butter knife with silver blade and stained ivory handle by Peter and Anne Bateman, London. 1796. 8in. *(A)*

21 Butter knife with engraved silver blade and rectangular agate handle. George Unite, Birmingham. 1836. 8½in. *(A)*

22 Butter knife with silver scoop blade and bone handle by Joseph Willmore, Birmingham. 1810. 7½in. *(A)*

23 Sheffield plate snuffer scissors. 1835. 7in. *(A)*

24 Silver fiddle-pattern butter knife with cow engraving by Charles Boyton, London. 1871. 8in. *(A)*

25 Silver-gilt spoons made in Cologne; the smaller **(25a)** bears the mark of Peter Kaff. 1650–70. 7 and 7½in. Each *(D)*

26 Butter knife with stained ivory handle. 1800. 9in. *(A)*

27 Rare Scottish "Puritan" spoon with plain, plank-shaped stem. Only four such are known. 17th C. 5in. *(E/F)*.

28 Silver butter knife with curved blade **(28a)** and a gemstone inset at the end of the handle **(28b)**. 1900. 6in. *(C)*

29 Brass ashtrays inset with the faces of Oliver Cromwell and King Charles I **(29a)**. 19th C. 3in wide. Each *(A)*

30 Rare chest-shaped silver caddy with lock and key, by Robert Makepeace and Richard Carter of London. Chinese scenes on the sides **(30a)**. 1778. 3½in. *(G)*

31 Enniskillen (N. Ireland) town mace, bearing the town arms, the Irish harp, the rose of England and the arms of Queen Anne. 1706. 3ft 2in. *(G)*

32 French bronze Venus, a popular subject for Victorian statuary. 1890. 12in. *(D)*

33 One of a pair of silver vegetable dishes and covers with acanthus leaf decoration **(33a)**. Made by Paul Storr of London. 1794. 7in high. *(G)*

34 Silver-gilt salt by Paul Storr from a set of four **(34a–c)**. 1811–13. 5in. *(G)*

35 Silver "mosque" inkstand by Elkington & Co.; a presentation piece. 1898. 12in. *(G)*

39a

36 Silver candlestick, one of a set of two pairs. One pair **(36a)** made 1781, the other in 1787. 11in high. Set **(G)**

37 Silver match cases. Further examples **(37a–d)**. 1860–1910. 1–1½in. Each **(A)**

38 Victorian centerpiece for fruit with a cut and frosted glass dish on a silver stem of fruiting vines. 1869. 19in. **(E/F)**

39 Glass dish from a silver epergne **(39a)**; the glass dishes are interchangeable with candle sconces. 1835. 18in. **(G)**

40 Large Sheffield-made silver claret jug; one of a pair **(40a)**. When the handle is gripped, the lid opens automatically. 1898. 16in. Pair **(G)**

41 Child's spoon and pusher with distinctive handles. Made in Birmingham. 1914. 4in and 5in long. **(A)**

42 Gladiator, with sword held aloft **(42a)**, one of a pair made in Germany of spelter, a low-grade zinc alloy which can look like bronze but is not so heavy. 1910. 20in. **(B/C)**

43 Copper weathervane in the shape of a peacock. Made in the United States. *c.*1870–1910. 16in high. **(A)**

44 Inscribed brass figure of a deer, probably Middle Eastern. Detail of head **(44a)**. 19th C. 6in long. **(A)**

45 Boat-shaped silver fruit basket with fly-punching, a mechanical piercing technique ideal for mass production. 1890–1910. 12in long. **(D)**

46 Italian plaque in chased gold relief, mounted on lapis with cornelians at the corners. Made for the Borghese family by Gugliemo della Porta as part of a cabinet. 16th C. 10in. **(G)**

47 American Rookwood earthenware jug with electroplated pattern of flowers and foliage in silver. 1890. 6in. **(D)**

48 Machine-made silver bonbon dish with an enamel center in a medieval style **(48b)**. The hammer marks on the base **(48a)** were added later. 1908. 4in diameter. **(C)**

49 Electroplated silver gondola rosebowl with original glass liner and grill. Made in Germany. 1900. 16in. **(G)**

50 Ornate silver match case with ridged striker on the bottom. Late 19th C. 1½in. **(A)**

51 Dutch marriage casket in silver, engraved with scenes of courting couples. In very fine condition. 1630. 3in long. **(G)**

52 Detail from a bronze group "Monkey Steeplechase" **(52a)** by Paul-Joseph Gayrard, Paris. 1850. 10in long. **(E)**

53 Front and rear view **(53a)** of a silver figure of a chauffeur. The base **(53b)** bears a Chester hallmark, but it was most probably made in Birmingham. 1906. 4in. **(D/E)**

54 Novelty brass match case modeled on the British prime minister William

36a

Gladstone. Late 19th C. 2½in. **(A)**

55 Child's miniature silver tea and coffee service. 1905. Tray 6in. **(C)**

56 Sugar bowl from silver tea set in a Japanese style, reflected in the exotic shape. Teapot **(56b)**. Milk jug **(56a)**. Detail of handle **(56c)**. 1879. Teapot 5in high. **(E)**

57 French or Florentine classical-style bronze after a marble original of Belvedere Antinous; paired with a Medici Venus. Late 17th C. 20in high. **(G)**

58 Electroplated teapot and milk jug **(58a)**, part of a French service by Frenais. 1880. Teapot 9½in. Pair **(B)**

59 Silver tankard with pomegranate feet and thumbpiece. The inscription on the base **(59a)** records its presentation in 1662 to British envoy Sir Philip Meadows. 16in high. **(G)**

60 Scandinavian silver spice container. 19th C. 3in. **(A)**

61 Rare pair of silver teapots, made by Robert Garrard in late 18th-century style. The lids are engraved "green" **(61a)** and "bohea" for green and black tea. 1822. 5in. Pair **(F)**

62 "Man against Nature," French bronze statue on a marble base of a man wrestling a lioness. 1880. 2ft. **(E/F)**

63 Silver caudle cup made by Robert Sanderson in Boston, America, possibly for a wedding. A caudle cup was used for making hot gruel. Mid-17th C. 5in high. **(G)**

64 Rare silver-gilt vinaigrette made after the Battle of Trafalgar. A bust of Nelson is engraved on the front and the cast-and-pierced grille shows the *Victory*. 1805. 1½in. **(G)**

65 Electroplated tea caddy with a beautifully engraved lid **(65a)** and neoclassical swags. 1880. 5in high. **(A)**

66 George IV bronze and copper urn. The legs **(66a)** have animal feet and mask faces at the top, the handles **(66b)** are in the form of a dragon's head. 1830. 15in high. **(B)**

67 Oval silver tray with "rayed" effect; the reeded edge encloses a decorated border. 1870–80. 23½in. **(F)**

68 Silver sugar caster made in London. The style, but not the decoration **(68a)**, mimics 1740s style. 1898. 7in. **(B/C)**

69 Silver copy of a mid-18th-century three-legged sauce boat with engraved monogram. 1888. 5½in. **(C)**

70 Complete Sheffield-made box of flatware with silver handles. The knives **(70a)** have steel blades and the forks **(70b)** two steel prongs. 1770–80. Knife 9½in. Set **(F)**

71 Irish silver copy of a mid-19th-century rococo revival tea set with typically ornate decoration, particularly the scroll work and the female figure on the teapot **(71b)**. Detail of handle **(71a)**. 1915. Teapot 6in high. Set **(G)**

52a

PRICE CODE: **A** less than $200 **B** $200–400 **C** $400–750 **D** $750–1,500 **E** $1,500–3,000 **F** $3,000–5,000 **G** over $5,000

THE END OF THE HUNT

WONDERS OF SCIENCE

1 The pantograph (14) was used to copy maps. By adjusting the hinges the image could be either enlarged or reduced at will.

2 At sea, the sextant (12) or octant (23), used with a chronometer (30), determines latitude and longitude. The orrery (2) could provide space travelers with a guide to our solar system. The surveyor's or miner's dial (20) indicates direction without points of visual reference.

3 The block instrument (1) used telegraphic messages to determine whether a railway line was clear. The nautical telescope (6), with inset flag guide, was essential for reading signals at sea.

4 The collection of weather guides (5) was used by the British polar explorer Robert Falcon Scott (1868–1912) on his fatal expedition to the Antarctic in 1910. The worn ebony and brass octant (23) assisted in the search for Sir John Franklin, the explorer who was lost while trying to find the Northwest passsage.

5 A compass (4a, 5b) is essential for finding direction. The ivory draftsman's rule (24) is an elegant measure of distance. Two sets of balance beam scales (10, 18) provide accurate weight readings. Thermometers (4b, 5) measure temperature.

6 The Edison phonograph (15) brought music into the home and gave pleasure to thousands. The best views at the opera could be enhanced through a pair of opera glasses (11, 21). Restful birdsong would have come from the singing birds in the gilded cage (3).

7 They are all kinds of barometer using different methods to measure air pressure and so predict the weather. The stick barometer (7, 17, 22) uses a column of mercury to register pressure change. The aneroid barometer (4c, 5d) has a partial vacuum chamber to detect changes in pressure and was developed for use at sea. The wheel barometer (8) also uses a mercury tube, but achieves a more accurate result by activating a pointer. These were also known as banjo barometers because of their shape.

8 The military surgeon's kit (19) brought help to those injured in the trenches of WWI.

BLUE-AND-WHITE BAZAAR

1 The Ming pen tray (39) would grace any desk. The ewer and basin (64) was a bathroom feature before running hot water. The quintal vase (58), invented in Holland, brought bulbs into the home. The salt (30) takes its name from the condiment it holds.

2 The daikon, or white radish, appears in the Hirado pottery (4).

3 The willow pattern, a standard design emulating Chinese style, was actually invented in Britain in the late 18th century. Examples can be seen on plates (3, 17, 59) and the spirit decanters (42). The pattern on plate 17c has been reversed.

4 The ordinary-looking tea bowl (11) made in the 15th century was sold for approximately $500,000.

5 Both have decorative uses. A garniture (49) is used to embellish or "garnish" a mantelpiece. The lambrequins, a scalloped decoration, are used to decorate the edges of cups (26) and plates.

6 The Florian vases (24) were inspired by jugs found at the Roman town of Pompeii. Porcelain-makers Sitzendorf have attempted to pass themselves off as their rival Meissen by using a similar mark (72).

7 Spirit decanters, labeled "W" for whisky (42a) and "B" for brandy (42b), capture the spirit of Scotland and fire of France.

8 Plate 32 has a portrait of the British prime minister William Gladstone, who gave his name to the Gladstone bag.

9 The Spode plate (65) depicts oxen and a camel in an exotic landscape, a scene not normally associated with blue and white.

10 A sedate tea drinker can be seen on a teapot (55); the golfer teeing off (48d) is on a plate (48).

MYSTERIES OF THE EAST

1 The moonflask (18) was made in England by Minton. The elegant jardinière (14), by Christofle, is French and the Japanese-style tea set (15) was made in the United States by Gorham.

2 The embroidered panel (20) was made in Turkey, then considered part of the orient. The bridge cloth (8) is Indian and the wall hanging (35, 64) was made in Japanese.

3 Cloisonné (12) creates a pattern by inlaying different types of colored enamels into wires soldered onto a metal vessel. Parquetry (14, 17, 26) inlays other materials into a wooden background. Shibayama (22) creates a pattern by inlaying different materials into a base metal such as iron or bronze.

4 Traditional Japanese clothing lacks the pockets found in western dress and so the inro (11, 37) is used for small personal possessions. It comprises a series of compartments secured by a cord and a decorative toggle known as a netsuke (6, 31). The okimono (11, 37) is a carved figure, used for household decoration.

5 Until the end of the 18th century it was cheaper for westerners to order decoration. The work table (25) was made especially for western markets, as there were no such items in the East.

6 The fisherman (24) was carved from an ivory tusk. The Swiss-made watch (33) was lacquered with cinnabar, which is made from elephant ivory and stand on an ivory and returned to Europe.

7 Magnificent cranes appear on an ivory and stand on such items in the East. The geese appear on pieces 34 and 19. The elephant cranes appear on the wings.

8 The ebony elephant (39), at $15,000–$22,500, is the most valuable. The box (29), topped by an eagle, is made from a stag-antler leaf. The beetle box (23) is decorated with crushed beetle wings.

9 The god Hotei plays Go with a young boy inside, with inlaid shibayama ball is the most valuable, a tiny wood carving (32).

COUNTRY STYLE

1 The paneled oak chest (49) was made as a blanket box. The two commodes (14, 63) conceal chamber pots beneath lift-up seats. The raised chest (36), called a doughboy, kept baker's dough in good condition. Pine can be seen in

2 Country furniture used readily available woods. Pine can be seen in dressers (19, 21), chests (22, 61) and tables (67); oak in benches (29), boxes (37, 49, 50), dressers (38, 62), bedsteads (43) and tables (45); and beech in chairs (16, 32).

3 The canterbury (40) was used in the 18th century as a plate-holder. In the 19th century it stored sheet music.

4 Although samplers fulfill a decorative function (35, 64), they were originally created as a catalog of stitches (39).

5 The table (10) is considered to be one of the finest examples of the work of the Shaker religious community, renowned for its craftsmanship. The other two are a set of drawers (52) and a rocking chair (15).

6 The Orkney chair (27) was made from driftwood as there are no trees on the island. The small drawer was used for tobacco and whisky.

7 The Windsor chair (28) was made with desk extension in the United States.

JEWELRY BOX

1 The dragonfly is on a diamond and peridot brooch (65), the "fairy" is 10. The lion is on a mother-of-pearl cameo (112) and the dove (87a) is a detail of the Pliny's Doves brooch (87).

2 The gemstone associated with seas and oceans is the aquamarine. It is found in the diamond pendant (100), the diamond brooch (98) and earring (95a).

3 The torpedo cuff links (15, 15a) are by Peter Carl Fabergé (1846–1920).

4 Both the 19th-century plaque (28), made from shell cameo, and the 19th-century bangle (27), in gold and mosaic, depict this scene from classical mythology.

5 The gold turtle brooch (86) carries a pearl on his back and the oval locket (11) is made from a hawksbill turtle shell.

6 The good luck wishbone brooch (37) could have been plucked from a chicken.

WHATNOTS TO WARDROBES

1 Both are found on drawer fronts and panels. Stringing refers to thin strips of wood inlaid as a decoration (4) and cross-banding (39) runs at right angles to the grain of the main wood, to form a border.

2 There are many to choose from: writing slopes (48, 59), davenports (30, 55), secretaire-bookcases (10, 11a, 43, 56), roll-top desks (21, 51), secretaires (1) and writing tables (13, 22).

3 Ormolu, literally "milled gold," is the term used for gilded bronze common on French furniture of the 18th century (22, 35, 50).

4 The American dressing table (28) is painted. The Italian cabinet (12) has been inlaid with ivory. Stainless steel banding can be seen on the Art Deco sideboard (5); brass bands decorate the wine cooler (40) and gilt plaques adorn the credenza (50).

5 A whatnot (16) is a set of display shelves. A credenza (50) is a buffet or sideboard for the display and serving of food. The linen press (54) is a forerunner of the wardrobe.

6 "Federal" refers to furniture made in the United States from 1790 to 1830, adopting European styles such as Hepplewhite, Sheraton and Empire. Other Federal pieces include 28 and 34.

TABLES AND CHAIRS

1 Chippendale-style chairs (2, 36) were rarely made by Thomas Chippendale (1718–79) but taken from his guide 'The Gentleman and Cabinet Maker's Director,' published in 1754. As its name suggests, the gothic-style chair (12) has a printed arch design on the back. The Federal chair (31) is an American adaptation of a European chair style. The Hepplewhite-style chair (22), like most of Hepplewhite's (d.1786) furniture, is characterized by simplicity and elegance.

2 This table and chair (10) is made from papier mâché, but would have been strong enough to support sewing work.

3 Checkers, backgammon and cribbage are associated with the carved games table (34). The card game too would be played on the card table (50). The elegant teapoy (7) would have supported a kettle while tea was served. The kettle stand (18), also used as a wine stand, served the same purpose. The unusual Monxman table (6). Poker or bridge would be played on the card table.

4 The confidante (8) allowed two people to conduct an intimate conversation and the nursing chair (28) was used by Victorian mothers when feeding their babies.

5 The occasional table (27) has a lyre-shaped support.

6 The furniture designers of the 19th century used buttoning on chair backs (3, 13, 23).

7 The folding chair (57) could easily be moved and would have been used in the garden.

CHINA CLOSET

1 The Wedgwoods have captured their home (35) and a metallic effect (13) in teapots. Flora and fauna, a cabbage and a snake, are provided by a French teapot (21).

2 The Worcester tureen is hand-painted (11), the Sunderland ewer (72) is printed with verses and pictures, the Wedgwood teapot and the wickerwork is on the Belleek teapot (54).

3 Oysters are eaten from the majolica dish (23); the Worcester candlestick provides light (18), coffee is being drunk in a porcelain tableau (40) and St. Lucy gives away the function of the majolica drug jar (36).

4 The conservatory seat (22) is ancient Egyptian. Vases in the Greek style (26, 26a) show the Victorian passion for things classical. The majolica plate (76) is renaissance and the cherub and ornate decoration make the spill-holder (65) rococo.

5 Characters from the Commedia dell' Arte represent the theatre (24); the Cheshire Cat (46) from Lewis Carroll's Alice in Wonderland represents literature; and characters from Walt Disney's The Lady and the Tramp (52, 52a) represent the film.

6 The Rockingham mug (69) depicts a mail wagon; sailing ships ply their way on a ewer and basin illustration (72), and a commemorative plate portrays a flying boat (9).

7 The matt effect of saltglaze (35, 45) is obtained by throwing salt into the kiln when it is at its hottest. Parian (75) is a hardpaste porcelain developed to resemble marble. Slipware (31) is decoration in raised relief added to the unfired pottery as a creamy paste or slip.

GLASS

1 The rolling pin (7) has been blown into shape, with transfers added to the inside. The shoe-shaped salt and pepper holder (30) has been machine-pressed to resemble cut glass, a process popular in the 19th century. The molded bust of Napoleon III (28) was made as a memento of the 19th century. The emperor, who died in 1873. The trumpet (27) was formed by drawing the heated glass to the required length.

2 Overlay work in silver can be seen on the Loetz vase (10) where a layer of silver was built up by electrolysis then partly cut to reveal the glass. The overlaid blue-colored glass on the decanter (14a) was cut to reveal the clear glass beneath. Cameo glass can be seen on the two lampshades (4, 36). It is made of two different layers of glass; one is then cut back to create a design in relief. The decoration on the souvenir beaker (42) is painted with enamels.

3 Decalcomania refers to the craze for colored transfers; a prime example of this art form is the decorated rolling pin (7).

4 Italian makers Marius Sabino produced a figurine (39) resembling a famous piece – "Suzanne" – by French glass designer René Lalique (31).

5 The candlestick (22) is a frigger piece, made by press-molding leftover glass, or frigger. Carnival glass (13, 16, 34) was first manufactured as Taffeta or Nancy glass in 1907, but the name changed when it became a popular prize at carnivals and funfairs.

6 A rummer (6, 32) was used especially for rum but for ale or cider. The goblet (25) was made not for wine but for ale or cider. The barley and hop motifs on the ale glass (41) give away its use. The cordial glass (15) was used for fruit liqueurs.

7 Rare Tiffany lava glass pieces (37) can realize prices in excess of $30,000 each.

QUESTION TIME

1 The well-protected carriage clock (49) was designed for rough traveling. A special device repeated the last hour struck, telling the time even in the pitch dark.

2 Contrary to expectation, the inner workings of the "mystery clock" (47) are concealed in the clock, not the figurine; the face moves with the pendulum.

3 The mantel clock (54) plays a repertoire of familiar tunes; the red marble clock (53) is shaped like a classical lyre; the Dresden china clock (50) has a painted muse of music and plays a tune.

4 Both features are found on tall case clocks (14, 52). A spandrel is the space between the dial and square mount. The lenticle is a window which exposes the pendulum.

5 The hunter watch was designed to withstand the rigors of the fox hunt, with a protective cover for the watch glass. Two are shown here; the full hunter (17) and the half-hunter (27), which has a small hole for telling the time without opening the watch.

6 The 1930s Piguet wristwatch (11) is the most valuable at $100,000.

7 The flick clock (8) was commonly known as the "Every Ready Plato."

8 The rococo style (1720–70) is emulated by the gilt-brass mantel clock (46). The straight lines of the classical period (1775–1810) are copied in some tall case clocks (14, 52). The tall case clock (35) represents the gothic style (1830–80). The pierced clock (72) is in the Art Nouveau style (1895–1920) and the diamond watch (10) in Art Deco (1910–25).

9 The waterfall clock (12) has a revolving glass rod, simulating running water. The leopard's eyes move from side to side to echo the pendulum on clock 48.

10 The early English watch (6) has only one main hand because precise time-keeping was not necessary in the 17th century. The Patek Philippe watch (51) has a dial showing phases of the moon.

11 The tall case clock (1) was never unpacked! The pine casing was protective packaging rather than for display.

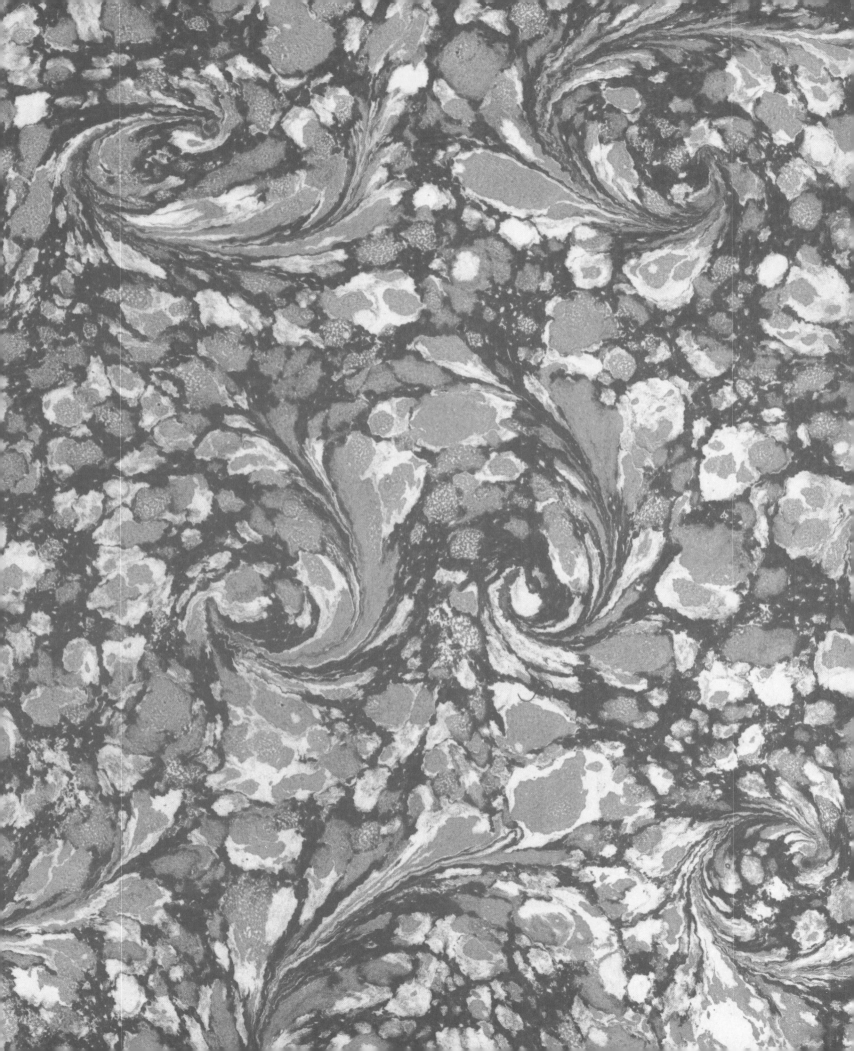